BROADCAST GRAPHICS

ON THE SPOT

Time-Saving Techniques Using Photoshop and After Effects for Broadcast and Post Production

by Richard Harrington

Glen Stephens

Chris Vadnais

DV Digital Video
EXPERT SERIES

CMP**Books**

San Francisco

Published by CMP Books
an imprint of CMP Media LLC
600 Harrison Street, San Francisco, CA 94107 USA
Tel: 415-947-6615; fax: 415-947-6015
www.cmpbooks.com email: books@cmp.com

Series Editor: Richard Harrington
Managing editor: Gail Saari
Cover design: Damien Castaneda, David Hamamoto

Distributed to the book trade in the U.S. by: Distributed in Canada by:
Publishers Group West   Jaguar Book Group
1700 Fourth Street   100 Armstrong Avenue
Berkeley, CA 94710   Georgetown, Ontario M6K 3E7 Canada
1-800-788-3123   905-877-4483

For individual orders and for information on special discounts for quantity orders, please contact:
CMP Books Distribution Center, 6600 Silacci Way, Gilroy, CA 95020
Tel: 1-800-500-6875 or 408-848-3854; fax: 408-848-5784; email: cmp@rushorder.com; Web: www.cmpbooks.com

ISBN: 1-57820-273-6

05 06 07 08 09   5 4 3 2 1

Dedications

This book is dedicated to Larry, Jack, John, Dave, and Eric for teaching an impatient guy a whole lot. Your early patience has set the stage for so much more.
—Richard Harrington

This book is dedicated to Ellen Pence for giving me the freedom at work to learn, teach, and influence this industry and Matt Petrowsky for always challenging me to think outside the box.
—Glen Stephens

This book is dedicated to the Air Force Broadcasting Service for promoting education and training, and for giving me the time and flexibility to write, teach, and learn in the civilian broadcast industry. Special thanks to my mentors Harry Lockley and Bill Hickman, who make things look so easy.
—Chris Vadnais

Contents

With improvements in both keying technology and cameras, it is possible to get professional results on tighter budgets.

Being creative takes time, but the whole reason behind computers was so we could drive those flying cars, have robots serve us, and work those 15 hour work weeks.

Being original is an important of your design abilities. Being done is a more important expression of your desire to keep your "high-paying" job.

You'll likely be putting a client's brand on the screen quite often. In this chapter we'll take a look at some easy ways to do that.

It's one of the most important elements in a newscast. It reinforces, explains, or somehow drives the message your news anchor is trying to communicate.

Effects can catch your audiences eye as well as set you apart from the competition.

Working in Photoshop and After Effects is great, but those two programs are merely the beginning of your graphic's journey.

Introduction

Why did we write this book? Well we thought it would be good to get this information out there. When we started in broadcasting, information was scarce (but at least there was still some sort of apprenticeship system in place). Even today, it's hard to find the right information, especially when you're always "on deadline."

So we wrote a book. The idea was to give the reader the cream off the top of the milk—just the good stuff. Adobe Photoshop and After Effects are great programs, with tons of features and shortcuts; the problem is separating the cream from the skim milk.

If you read every tech document on the web, perused every page of the manual, attended all of the Adobe courses, frequented online forums, and hung out with all the other Adobe uber-geeks, you'd have a bounty of knowledge (trust us, we have and we do). But you have a life, a job, and no time to dig to find those gems.

If you're impatient, on a deadline, or just can't stand to look at another "Getting Started" book, this book is for you.

We've all used these programs to create real work that has had real airtime. We've collectively produced content for news, entertainment, commercial, corporate, and government applications, while meeting our deadlines along the way. Being fast and creative have been essential traits to remaining gainfully employed.

Who Is This Book For?

If you work in television, this book is for you. If you create graphics for work that shows on televisions, this book is for you. If you think producing 80 graphics in an eight-hour day means things were light...then this book is still for you (but some of it you'll already know because of your superior stamina and intellect).

If you've never opened the manual, read another Photoshop and After Effects book, or taken a training class, don't start here. You must learn to walk before you can run. If you're a "newbie," this book may leave you a bit overwhelmed. Buy it anyway, but read it after you've had some walking lessons.

With that said, don't try to read the book linearly. Shop for ideas, jump around a lot, and work your way through the chapters you need most. We've left extra space by the tips so you can jot down your own notes. If you're a mobile designer or editor, this book should fit nicely in your bag. Hit a tough spot, and just pull the book out to check for a new idea or a troubleshooting tip—when the client leaves the room, of course. Have a few minutes to kill, read a tip. We bet you'll return with some new ideas and new energy.

If you're looking for the little sidebars or tips in the margins, there aren't any. This whole book is filled with more than 300 tips. Get reading already—you've got a deadline to make.

—Richard Harrington, Glen Stephens, and Chris Vadnais

Updates

Want to receive e-mail updates for *Broadcast Graphics On the Spot?* Visit our web site **www.cmpbooks.com/ maillist** and select from the desired categories. You'll automatically be added to our preferred customer list for new product announcements, special offers, and related news.

Your e-mail address will not be shared without your permission, so sign up today!

Acknowledgments

My wife, Meghan, for her patience and love. You are an amazing person, and there are times I cannot believe you put up with my crazy jobs. As we move through life, I am grateful you are by my side.

My son Michael, you make me laugh. It is wonderful to watch you grow up. You teach me so much and make me a better man. Thank you for your "helpful" tech support while trying to write this book.

My family for their support and guidance. All that I have, I owe to you. Thanks for all of the good advice and teaching throughout the years.

—Richard Harrington

To my wife, Sabra, thank you for enabling and supporting me to work on this project. Your selflessness and commitment to me, my career, and our family is divine. Thank you for your understanding and patience with all of the time I spend working. I could not do it without the most important person in my life; you.

To my kids, Brandon and Ashlee, thank you for helping me to keep things in perspective and realize sometimes you just need to have fun! You keep me young (and running)! Being your dad is the most fulfilling job I have.

To my parents, thank you for supporting all of my endeavors and helping me to believe that there isn't anything I can't do. The commitment that you have shown to me, my education, and my development as an individual have made me who I am today.

—Glen Stephens

To my wife Amy, thank you for providing the support and encouragement I need to accomplish my goals. Without you I would be forever in doubt.

To my son Zade, thanks for being so much fun. Your sense of humor is perfect. Set your goals high; you can do anything you want.

To Jerry Shields, your support is unique, and over time has become imperative. Thanks for absorbing my rants and providing honest feedback. I can always count on you.

—*Chris Vadnais*

The authors would like to thank the following for making this book possible:

Gary Adcock	Ben Kozuch
Dorothy Cox	*Layers Magazine*
DV Magazine	Dave Legg
DVPA	Dominic Milano
Eric Fishback	John Pascuzzi
Marcus Geduld	*Photoshop User Magazine*
Rod Harlan	Kimberly Reed
Jayse Hansen	Gail Saari
Larry Hawk	Abba Shapiro
KCCI	Paul Temme
Scott Kelby	Jack Tow
Steve Kilisky	

ON THE SPOT

Up and Running
Configuring Software for Maximum Performance

Designing graphics for a broadcast environment is pretty demanding stuff. Between the deadlines, technical challenges, and "talent issues," it can get pretty stressful. While we can't retrain your co-workers, we can help you refine your software.

It's important to get your system tuned and ready to go. This chapter offers several tips on configuring your system. These tips are based on our workflows and experience—use the ones that make sense, skip others if they don't fit your needs. But be prepared to look at your work a little differently.

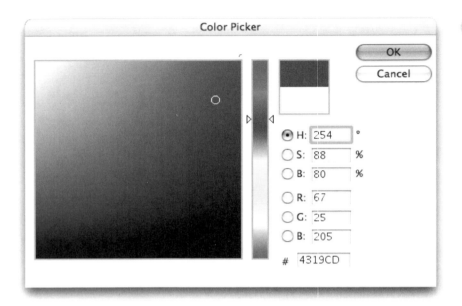

Consistent Color

Need to get precise color choices? Then be sure to use the Adobe Color Picker. By default this is the one that both Photoshop and After Effects use.

Both programs will allow you to use RGB or HSB color. You can also use hex colors if the web is more familiar to you. If you need to access Pantone colors (such as for ad work) you can access that in Photoshop from within the color picker.

UI Font Size

It might be the fact that monitors keep getting higher resolution (or maybe we're just getting old). Text just seems to keep getting harder to read. Under Photoshop CS2, it's finally an option to change the user interface font size.

1 Press Cmd+K (Ctrl+K) to call up the Photoshop General preferences.

2 Choose to set the UI font size to Small, Medium, or Large.

3 Restart Photoshop CS2 for the change to take effect.

Tool Tips Give Psychic Powers

You know how much pros on a deadline depend upon keyboard shortcuts. But how do they learn them? Is there a secret club? Well yes... but we're allowed to tell you about Tool Tips nonetheless.

You'll find Tool Tips in both Photoshop and After Effects on the General tab. Be sure to turn this option on. Now when you rollover an unknown or infrequently used tool, you'll get useful information (including the keyboard shortcuts).

A Faster Toolbox

You've gone through the effort to learn all of the keyboard shortcuts for Photoshop. Now let's make them faster. From the General Preferences tab, uncheck Use Shift Key for Tool Switch. Now, instead of having to use two keys to switch tools, you can now just tap the letter to cycle through all of the tools in a well. For example, tap M to switch between the Elliptical and Rectangular Marquee.

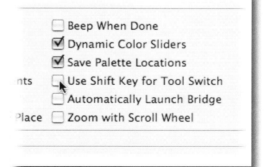

A Good Place

With Photoshop CS2, we gain a substantial new ability. Placed objects remain as Smart Objects, giving you the ability to access all of the original raster data. This essentially allows you to size and resize an object repeatedly without quality loss.

❶ Choose File>Place... (this just screams to be remapped to a keyboard shortcut).

❷ Navigate to the object you want to add (it must be a compatible graphics format)

❸ Certain file formats (such as multi-page PDFs) may offer an additional dialog box with self-explanatory options.

❹ Adjust the scaling of the placed object using your mouse or the Options Bar.

❺ Click the checkbox or press Enter twice.

You can now scale up the object to its original raster size or even infinitely if it is a vector object as Photoshop reads in the original data. You can also edit the original object by double-clicking the smart object thumbnail in the Layers palette.

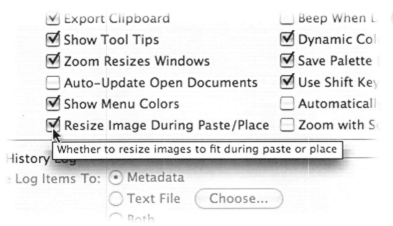

A Better Place

Needless to say, Place will become part of your regular workflow. Lets make it even faster!

❶ Press Cmd+K (Ctrl+K) to call up your Photoshop preferences.

❷ From the General preferences tab, choose Resize Image During Paste/Place. This will save you some time, as the placed image will scale down to fit inside your document window.

❸ Click OK and starting placing.

A Better Workspace

You've achieved interface nirvana... the windows and palettes are perfectly arranged, just how you need them. You can quickly find just what you need and the software feels more intuitive... so save it! Workspaces allow you to save palette locations and window views. This is the fastest way to switch between tasks as you can arrange all of the tools into optimum workspaces.

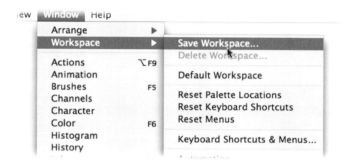

❶ Arrange your windows and palettes to taste.

❷ Choose Window> Workspace> Save Workspace.

❸ Give the Workspace a name that is descriptive.

❹ You may want to quit and re-launch the application. Workspaces are stored with your preferences, which are written when Photoshop or After Effects is cleanly quit. A crash would result in your settings not being stored.

How to Handle your Files

Photoshop supports a lot of different file formats, we often find it hard to keep them all straight. Computers use two and three letters after a file name to denote the file type. This extension helps the computer properly open up the files by telling the computer how to interpret the data inside. Instead of having to remember a bunch of two and three letter codes, allow Photoshop to do this for you.

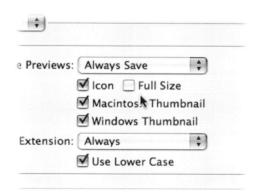

From the File Handling Preference tab

- Choose Always Append File Extensions and Use Lower Case. This will append the proper code at the end.

- While you're there, you may also want to check Always Save Image Previews. Icon and Thumbnails are usually enough, unless you are doing desktop publishing work.

Zoom... Zoom

It may be time to get a new mouse... one with a Scroll Wheel. Starting with Photoshop CS2 and After Effects 6.5, you gain the ability to zoom right from the mouse.

	☑ Dynamic Color Sliders
ndows	☑ Save Palette Locations
n Documents	☑ Use Shift Key for Tool Switch
s	☐ Automatically Launch Bridge
ring Paste/Place	☑ Zoom with Scroll Wheel

Determines if zooming or scrolling is the default wheel action

ta

Photoshop

❶ Press Cmd+K (Ctrl+K) to call up the General preferences.

❷ Select the Zoom With Scroll Wheel option to enable this behavior.

❸ Select the Zoom Tool (Z).

❹ Scroll the wheel to zoom in or out.

After Effects

Nothing special to change, the behavior works by default as long as you are over the Comp Window. But it doesn't stop there.

In the Timeline Window:

- Scroll – This will scroll up and down in the Timeline.

- Option + Scroll (Alt+Scroll) – This will zoom in or out on the Timeline.

- Shift + Scroll – This will Scroll Left or Right in the Timeline.

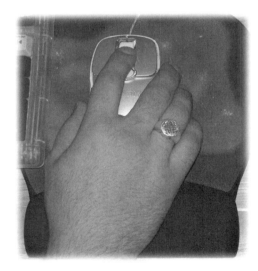

Innovate Safely

If the entire world all switched to the latest version of Photoshop at the same, our lives would be a lot easier. But that's not ever going to happen (although it sure would make Adobe happy if it did).

Oftentimes you're going to have to share files with other users. It is possible to open up newer PSD files in older versions of Photoshop. Now keep in mind, not all features will transfer, but it's a start. From the File Handling Preference tab check the box next to Maximize PSD and PSB File Compatibility.

Better Cursors

Accuracy is an important thing if you want to create video graphics. In fact it's practically a job requirement. Your tools in Photoshop can be way more accurate and give you better results.

From the Displays & Cursors Preferences tab:

- For Painting Cursors, choose to see a normal brush tip. This will make tasks such a layer masking even easier. Under Photoshop CS2, choose the new option to see a Full Size Brush Tip. You can also choose to add Show Crosshair in Brush Tip.

- For your Other Cursors, go with precise. A crosshair is much more accurate than a cute icon when sampling colors with the eyedropper.

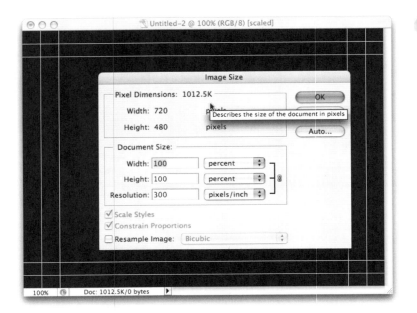

Video Graphics are NOT 72 dpi

Despite popular opinion, video graphics are not measured in dots per inch or pixels per inch (that is for print only). Video graphics are the same amount of pixels whether they are going to Dick Tracy's wristwatch or to the screen at your local sports bar. Computer monitors used to be 72ppi, but that changed with multi-resolution monitors.

For greater accuracy, measure your video graphics in pixels.

❶ Press Cmd+K (Ctrl+K) to call up your Photoshop preferences.

❷ Switch to the Units & Rulers preference tab.

❸ Set your Rulers to pixels. Greater accuracy and a bit more factual.

Type Options

The wayward sheep have finally found a home. Previously, Photoshop type preferences were scattered through several tabs and windows. Photoshop CS2 consolidates them into a new Preference tab. Be sure to set these preferences for maximum workflow.

- Use Smart Quotes – Will substitute true quote marks when you use the feet and inches key (the one next to Return/Enter).

- Show Font Names in English – Helpful for International and Dingbat fonts.

- Font Preview Size – Choose Medium or Large to cut down on squinting. Photoshop CS2 displays type in its actual face within the menu. This speeds up design decisions.

Guides, Grids, & Slices

Our sixth preference tab offers a few important choices. These aren't essential to change, but we find things work a little better when you modify these.

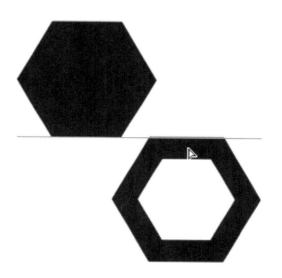

- Guides – These lines show up inside of Photoshop to mark you boundaries. Starting with Photoshop CS, they are also used to mark the title safe areas on the video templates.

- Smart Guides – These are new to Photoshop CS2, but are similar to what you'll find in Illustrator or DVD Studio Pro and Motion. When you start to drag an object, Smart Guides will highlight the edges or center to show alignment. Be sure to use a different color than your normal guides.

- Slices – Slices are for Internet rollover effects (such as navigation bars). They aren't very useful to you. Uncheck the box, Show Slice Numbers, to minimize accidentally turning slices on during video graphic design.

Color Management is for Printers

In Photoshop, the computer tries to simulate your output device on screen. In theory this is great... except in video there is no such thing as color management. A quick trip to the Electronics Department at Wal-Mart or Best Buy will show you how bad it is (look at 45 TVs turned to the same station and you'll get 45 different colored pictures). For Photoshop, it is important to turn Color Management Off.

❶ Press Cmd+Shift+K (Ctrl+Shift+K) to call up the Color Settings.

❷ Turn Color Management Off (Under CS2, you need the More Options button first).

❸ Now design away, when you bring the graphic into a video application like After Effects, Avid, Final Cut Pro, etc... you won't see a shift on your computer monitor. This however does not change the color variation when going from RGB space (the computer) to YUV (the video monitor). Be sure to use the Video Preview function to judge color accurately on your calibrated monitor.

Scratch Disks

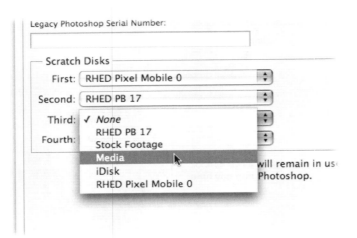

While it's not an every time thing, we run out of RAM when designing complex graphics. When this happens, Photoshop and After Effects turn to your scratch disk for virtual memory. Don't overlook this important setting, or your design session can come to a screeching halt. In fact, it's worth adding an extra internal drive if you've got an open slot.

In Photoshop:

❶ Press Cmd+K (Ctrl+K) to call up the Preferences window.

❷ Switch to the Plug-Ins and Scratch Disks tab or press Cmd+7 (Ctrl+7).

❸ Choose up to four Scratch Disks. Avoid using your startup volume if possible.

In After Effects: (6.5 and later)

❶ Press Cmd+Opt+; (Ctrl+Alt+;) to call up the Preferences window.

❷ Switch to the Memory & Cache tab.

❸ Check the Enable Disk Cache box.

❹ Set a Cache size in MB.

❺ Choose a folder on a hard disk (not a drive itself). Avoid using your startup volume if possible.

Full Screen Reposition

Photoshop offers three screen modes: Standard, Full with Menus, and Full. The second two are very useful when designing if you want to block out all of your floating windows (to limit your focus, or maybe that of the producer).

❶ From the Standard Screen Mode, press F twice to switch to Full Screen Mode.

❷ Press Cmd+= (Ctrl+=) to zoom in and make the picture larger.

❸ Hold down the space bar to get the hand tool... you can now position the full screen window better to accommodate your floating palettes.

❹ To eliminate the floating palettes press Tab. To eliminate all except your Toolbox and Options Bar press Shift+Tab.

❺ To restore the normal working view, press F once more and tab one or two times as needed.

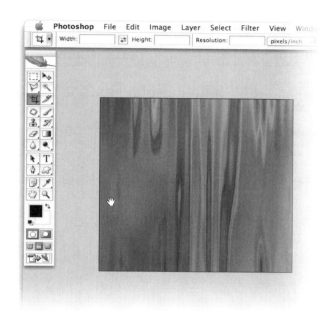

Scrolling Your Comp Window

A few versions ago, the After Effects team quietly killed off scroll bars in the Comp Window. This was done to make more space and clean up the interface. However a few people were stumped on how to move around. The solution is the hand tool. Just select the Comp Window you need to navigate and hold down the spacebar. You can now pan around the larger image and view as needed.

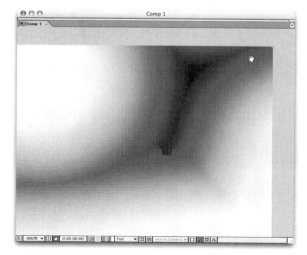

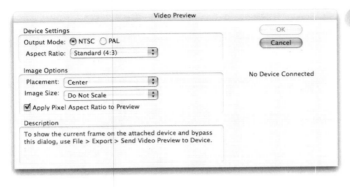

Use that Broadcast Monitor

Video graphics are meant to be seen on a video device. Otherwise a whole slew of issues can't be seen. It is essential to check for color, interlace flicker, and readability on a television or video monitor. Fortunately Adobe builds this into both applications starting with Photoshop CS2 and Adobe After Effects 6.5.

① Ensure the video device is connected and powered BEFORE launching Photoshop.

② Choose File>Export>Video Preview... The pop-up window will present you with logical choices (you can rollover an item for a detailed description).

③ Click OK. For subsequent previews, just choose File>Export>Send Video Preview to Device.

Arrange

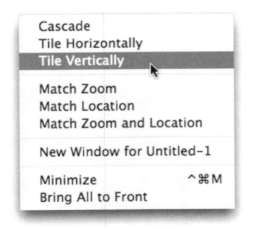

If you've got a lot of windows open at the same time, be sure to harness the power of Arrange (otherwise you'll waste a lot of time searching for things and playing shuffleboard). You have three choices in the Mac OS and four in Windows to organize your open documents.

- Cascade: Windows are stacked and cascade from the top left corner of the screen (much like a spread of cards). You can see each title bar and click on the document you want active.

- Tile Horizontally or Vertically: Images are arranged into a horizontal (or vertical) grid and fill the screen. Use the Zoom window option to make a window larger. Clicking the Zoom button a second time will return it to its place in the tile.

- Arrange Icons (Windows only): This minimizes the images and places them along the bottom edge of the screen. Click on the image you want to work with.

Use that Broadcast Monitor

With After Effects 6.5, preview out support is cross platform (and greatly improved). It is possible to preview the contents of a Layer, Footage, or Composition window on an external video monitor. All you need is a FireWire device such as a deck, camera, or DV Converter box.

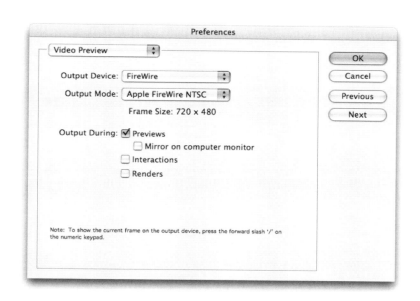

① Press Cmd+Option+; (Ctrl+Alt+;) to call up your preferences screen.

② From the Video Preview area, check the following options:

③ Select an Output Device – This will be FireWire for most users.

④ Choose an Output Mode – Pick which format your device supports. After Effects can output a DV50 signal if you have an appropriate device hooked up.

⑤ Choose one or more of the following interaction types:

- Previews: Both RAM preview and standard (i.e., using the spacebar) preview load on the external monitor.

- Interactions: Interactive previews, such as scrubbing and dragging in the Composition window on the external monitor.

- Renders: Each frame is shown the external monitor during a render. All renders are also mirrored.

You can toggle video output by pressing forward slash "/" on the numeric keypad. This is a great way to turn this handy feature on and off.

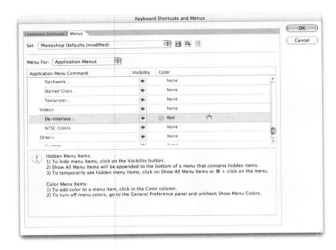

Edit Menus

In the quest to empower users, Adobe has unlocked menu customization in Photoshop CS2. This can be helpful to hide commands you never use (View Proof Colors>Working CMYK) to simplify the interface. You can also color code items to make them easier to find.

1. Choose Edit> Menus.

2. Pick an existing Set or create your own.

3. Choose to work with the Application or Palette Menus.

4. Click the visibility icon to hide any items you don't want access to.

5. You can also assign a color to certain commands you use most frequently.

6. Save your set and click OK.

7. If while working you need to see a hidden item, just choose Show All Menu Items from the bottom of the drop-down menu list.

Create New Layers at Best Quality

It used to be critical to work at draft quality throughout your After Effects design process (unless of course you wanted your computer to come to a grinding halt). But as processors have gotten faster and RAM cheaper, working with layers at Best Quality has become an important choice.

1. Press Cmd+Option+; (Ctrl+Alt+;) to call up your preferences screen.

2. From the General area, check the box next to Create New Layers At Best Quality.

3. Click OK.

This is an important timesaver, especially when working with effects such as glows or keying where accuracy in layer previews is essential.

Edit Keyboard Shortcuts

Starting with Photoshop CS, Adobe handed the ability to customize keyboard shortcuts to the end user. While this sounds extremely useful, you need to realize that several key combos are already in use.

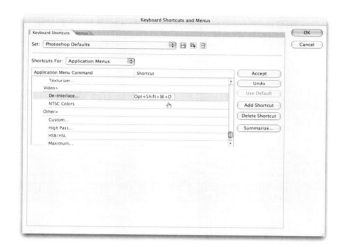

❶ Choose Edit> Keyboard Shortcuts.

❷ Pick an existing Set or create your own.

❸ You can work on Application Menus, Palette Menus, or Tools.

❹ Find a shortcut you want to modify (most not all are able to be changed- for example you can't make Quit, Cmd+S, to mess with your co-worker).

❺ Type a new keyboard shortcut, you'll need to use Cmd (Ctrl) or an F-key in the combo.

❻ If the combo is already taken, Photoshop warns you that you can either accept the change or pick a new one.

❼ Save your set and click OK.

Tabbed Windows Save Space

Is your monitor big enough? We suspect the answer is no (unless you own the 30-inch Apple HD display, then we secretly hate you). The key to working in After Effects is to keep similar windows grouped together.

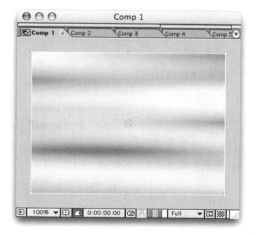

❶ Press Cmd+Option+; (Ctrl+Alt+;) to call up your preferences screen.

❷ From the General area, check the box next to Tabbed Windows.

❸ Click OK.

❹ Now, when you open multiple comps, the Timeline and Comp windows stay nested together. Just click on tabs to switch which comp is active. This is a HUGE space saver.

OpenGL Means Speed

If you've got a modern video card, chances are it supports the OpenGL standard. While OpenGL is best known for increased performance for gaming, you can harness its abilities for faster previews in After Effects.

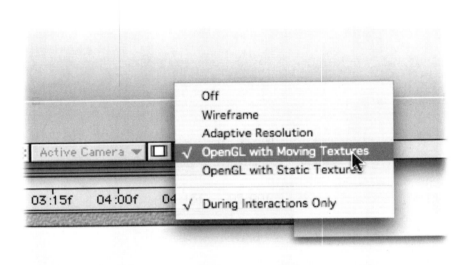

❶ Press Cmd+Option+; (Ctrl+Alt+;) to call up your preferences screen.

❷ From the Previews area, check the following options:

Enable Open GL – Turns your cards abilities on.

Effects use Adaptive Resolution when OpenGL is enabled – This allows the quality to drop for faster interactions when dragging sliders or moving elements.

Click OpenGL Info... and set the Quality to Faster.

Click OK.

❸ Click OK.

❹ From the Comp Window. click on the Fast Previews icon (it's the third one from the right edge along the bottom and looks like a comet).

❺ Choose OpenGL with Moving or Static Textures. Also specify that this is During Interactions Only. You do not want to use OpenGL for your static or RAM previews, only for dragging or other interactive adjustments.

Audio Preview – Lower Quality... Faster Previews

Sure you want audio in your previews, but there's no reason for it to take so long to load as well as to eat up RAM. In After Effects, lowering the preview quality of audio (especially if multiple tracks are involved) will give you a snappier response when you click Audio Preview or RAM Preview.

❶ Press Cmd+Option+; (Ctrl+Alt+;) to call up your preferences screen.

❷ From the Previews area, check the following options:

- Duration – Eight seconds is the default, we usually work with 10 or 15 seconds at a time.

- Sample Rate – This is only for Previews. For most computer speakers, 22 kHz is an imperceptible change.

- Sample Size – Lower from 16 Bit to 8 Bit.

- Channels- Unless you really need it, go for Mono previews.

❸ To preview the audio, place the current-time indicator at your start point.

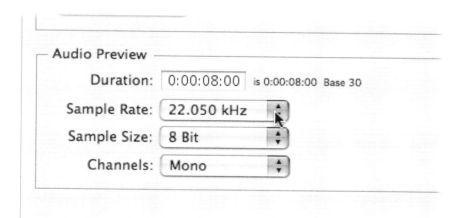

❹ Choose Composition>Preview>Audio Preview. (Here Forward) or press the period key on the numeric keypad.

If using the RAM Preview function to see audio and graphics, be sure the speaker icon is active in the Time Controls palette.

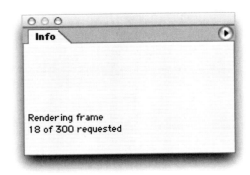

Keep Me Updated

If you're the type of user who wants to know what's going on at all times, then you need to modify After Effects a bit. One way to gauge how long certain design choices or effects take is to monitor their rendering info.

1 Press Cmd+Option+; (Ctrl+Alt+;) to call up your preferences screen.

2 From the Display area, check the box next to Show Rendering in Progress in Info Palette & Flowchart.

3 Click OK.

4 Call up the Info Palette by pressing Cmd+2 (Ctrl+2).

5 Engage a render or RAM preview and you will see After Effects scroll through info about which piece is rendering.

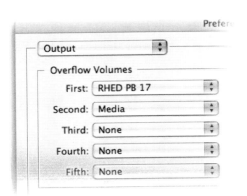

Overflow Volumes Save the Day

Have you ever returned to After Effects after a big batch render, only to discover that it was aborted due to a lack of space? This is a very frustrating way to miss a deadline, but can easily be prevented by a little bit of tweaking on your end.

1 Hook up an extra drive such as an external Firewire device or an internal drive or partition.

2 Press Cmd+Option+; (Ctrl+Alt+;) to call up your preferences screen.

3 From the Output area, choose up to five overflow volumes.

4 Specify a Minimum Diskspace Before Overflowing of at least 500 MB. Otherwise you can overfill and lock a disk.

5 Click OK and rest assured that After Effects will search out space for those big renders when it needs it.

Even Bigger RAM Previews

Sometimes when previewing a complex composition, we run out of RAM and the preview stops. Sure buying more RAM is an option if you've got the open slots as well as purchasing authority, but there's a more practical solution

① Press Cmd+Option+; (Ctrl+Alt+;) to call up your preferences screen.

② From the Memory & Cache area, check the following options:

Enable Disk Cache.

Maximum Disk Cache Size – 2000 MB adds about 2GB of virtual memory.

Choose Folder – You must specify an individual folder on a drive (or create a new cache folder). For best results, target a drive or partition other than your system drive.

③ Click OK.

④ Now when you RAM preview, After Effects will use hard disk space if it runs out of physical RAM.

A New Shade of Interface

Many video applications, such as Avid NLEs, Apple Shake, and Discreet combustion, ship with the interface set to 50 percent gray. This makes it easier to make complex judgments about color and contrast, and also cuts down on eye fatigue. After Effects 6.5 now gives you the ability to adjust the brightness of windows and palette backgrounds.

① Press Cmd+Option+; (Ctrl+Alt+;) to call up your preferences screen.

② From the User Interface Colors area, adjust the User Interface Brightness slider to adjust brightness.

③ Click OK.

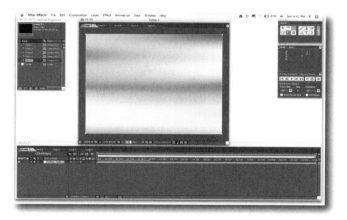

ON THE SPOT

Revealing Our Sources
Acquiring and Managing your Source Materials

The graphics you create for video productions will likely be composed of many different pieces of art and text. Some of these elements will come from your client (if you're lucky they'll even be high-res bitmaps or vector art), and others you will likely be expected to generate yourself. In this chapter we'll explore some ways to get high-quality image data into Photoshop.

Whether you're using a scanner or digital camera, saving a frame from a nonlinear editor, or creating images from scratch, these tips should help you save time and create the best-looking images possible. After all, this stuff is going to be on television! Now let's get started, your clients are waiting—and so is the TV audience!

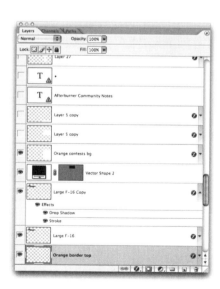

Ask and You Shall Receive (If You're Lucky)

A client who provides image data for you is doing two things. First, and most importantly to them, they're making sure you get their exact logo or font style. Branding is important; groups spend lots of money to create an image, which their logo represents. They won't (and shouldn't) settle for less than perfection.

Second, they're saving you time. Recreating a logo from scratch or repairing a tiny, blocky image designed for the web can be tedious work. Request the highest quality logo possible, and ask for vector art. This can include

- An Adobe Illustrator file (.ai)

- A vector encapsulated postscript file (.eps)

Many larger corporations have logos and resources available online in their "Press" areas. If you have to, ask to talk with the marketing/creative services people and ask them directly for vector art. Getting a high-quality logo to start with is a gift from the graphics gods, but sometimes you'll have to ask for it.

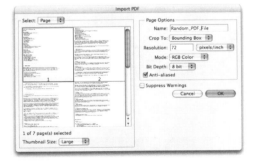

When the Well Runs Dry

If you're running out of luck in your search for high-quality image sources, check the PDF files. Many PDFs are built at print resolution and the artwork they contain may be suitable for video purposes with little manipulation.

❶ Choose File>Open.

❷ Navigate to the PDF file.

❸ Select the PDF, or select multiple docments by Cmd+clicking (Ctrl+clicking) on the filenames or thumbnails.

❹ Click OK.

Bring in the Vectors

Vector-based files will scale infinitely without creating nasty blocky edges. They're great to work with, and getting them into Photoshop is simple.

❶ Choose File>Open.

❷ Navigate to the vector file, select it, and click Open.

❸ A dialog box opens.

- Set the total pixel size as large as you need; be sure to measure in pixels.

- Ignore the resolution field.

- Set the Color Mode to RGB to ensure proper color handling.

When you accept the default values or specify your own, the file opens in its own new window. As soon as it opens in Photoshop, the illustration is rasterized, so go big in the Open options and scale down later to avoid those blocky edges.

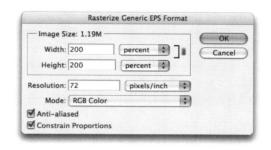

Importing EPS and AI Files into After Effects

Vector files are great for After Effects as well. The infinite scaling ability will come in handy for animation. However, this option is not on by default. When you add a vector element to your comp, be sure to turn on the Continuously Rasterize switch to ensure the smoothest scaling. After Effects will now read the vector data, giving you the best results.

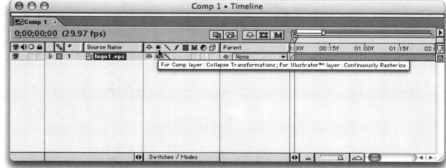

A Place for Everything

When working with vector art, you should strongly consider using the Place command, which drops the illustration right into your open document without asking any questions.

❶ Choose File>Place.

❷ Navigate to the vector file and click Place.

❸ The Image is added to your document with scaling handles attached.

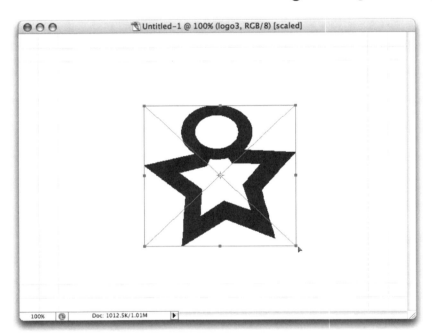

- Hold Shift when dragging to scale proportionally.

- Hold Option (Alt) when dragging to scale simultaneously from the center.

- These keystrokes can (and should) be combined for quick results that preserve proper aspect ratio. Speaking of aspect ratio, Photoshop CS automatically compensates for square pixels when placing a graphic element into a document using the video presets.

❹ The vector art is not rasterized until you hit Enter. This allows you to transform (even upscale) the vector art to your liking before Photoshop turns it into pixel data. This is handy if you don't know what size and resolution values you want to use and would rather "eyeball" it.

Simple Symbols and Shapes

The latest version of Adobe Illustrator ships with several vector-based symbols, which you can easily import to Photoshop. You will find more than 20 categories of symbols—everything from Food to International Currency. These often make great accents, bullets, or background pieces for full-screen slides. Save these ready-made vector graphics as AI files and import them to Photoshop using the Open or Place commands.

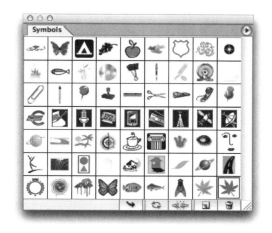

Photoshop CS can also create vector shapes. The Shape tool allows you to draw many different shapes, which it creates on a new layer. You can find even more shapes online at the Adobe Exchange (http://share.studio.adobe.com). Download and import these shapes to add them to your library.

1 Save the .csh file to your computer's Photoshop CS\Presets\Custom Shapes folder.

2 Open Photoshop CS.

3 Select the Custom Shape tool.

4 Expand the drop-down Shape selection window on the toolbar at the top of the screen.

5 Expand the submenu and click the name of the Custom Shape file you saved.

6 Select Append to add the new shape or set of shapes to your current shapes.

Be sure to backup your custom shapes (as well as other items in your presets folder.) When you ugrade (or reinstall) Photoshop, these presets are overwritten.

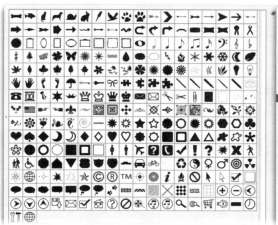

25

The Art of Scanning Art into Photoshop

Photoshop allows you to import images directly from your scanner. The driver that came with your scanner should be ready to work inside Photoshop. Check your scanner manufacturer's website frequently for software and driver updates.

❶ Select File>Import.

❷ If the scanner is properly installed and supported, the flyout menu should have a selection for it. Choose it.

❸ Your scanner's software interface pops up inside Photoshop, allowing you to select the areas to scan, set the resolution, and scan the image.

❹ When it's done, close your scanner's interface.

❺ The image is open in Photoshop, ready for adjustments.

Less (Resolution) is Moiré

Scanning images that were printed with a halftone method can produce an undesirable moiré pattern, especially if the scan is done in low resolution in a scanner's default mode. To avoid this, use your scanner's descreen setting. You should only use it when scanning certain printed images, though, as using a descreen setting when scanning photos produces blurry digital images. If your scanner doesn't have a descreen setting, Photoshop can help you get rid of the moiré pattern.

❶ Scan the image at high resolution.

❷ Use a Blur filter (Filters>Blur) to blur the scan just enough to clear the moiré pattern.

❸ Reduce the size of the image to match what you need (Image>Size).

❹ Refocus the image by applying the Unsharp Mask (Filter>Sharpen> Unsharp mask).

Size Does Matter

When scanning an image into Photoshop, you have the power to scan at various resolutions and sizes. The extra resolution really comes in handy, so make sure you scan images at a high resolution and size.

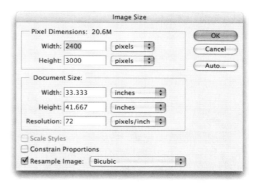

- Extra pixels come in handy when using tools like the Healing Brush.

- Higher-resolution files allow you to zoom in more before the image breaks up.

- Extra pixels allow you to crop the image later without having to upscale.

There is a LOT of misconception about how much to scan. To simplify, be sure to set your scanner to measure in total pixels. This is particularly important when scanning smaller images from letterheads or business cards. For a full-screen image, you'll want about 4,000 by 3,000 pixels (note the 4:3 ratio). Remember, you can always scale the image down without losing quality, so go ahead and create a larger file—just to be safe. If you plan to use the photo for pan-and-scan effects in After Effects, multiply your screen size by the amount of zoom you need. For example, for a 10X zoom you would need about 7,200 pixels of width by 4,800 pixels of height.

Go Ahead, Shoot

Digital cameras are ubiquitous, affordable, and compact enough for video professionals to carry on their person at all times. While you should generally be hesitant to use JPEG images, a decent digital camera (2.1 megapixels or more) set to its highest or "finest" setting will capture usable JPEGs. Use a digital camera to shoot a photo of a subject you want to use in your Photoshop composition. Most digital cameras now show up as removable drives in Windows and Macintosh operating systems. Simply plug the camera into the computer's USB port and select Open from the File menu to bring a photo into Photoshop from your USB camera. Once the files are transferred, be sure to convert them into a lossless file format such as TIFF or PICT. Convert them from JPEG as soon as possible to avoid permanently losing important image data in the compression.

Image Courtesy Nikon.

Unleashing Raw Power

Newer, moderately priced digital cameras allow you to take photos in RAW mode. This creates a sort of "digital negative" which has not been compressed or subjected to manipulation by the camera at all. Serious photographers have abandoned JPEG completely for the flexibility of the lossless RAW format. Photoshop CS allows you to open RAW files, and features a powerful interface for adjusting the photo.

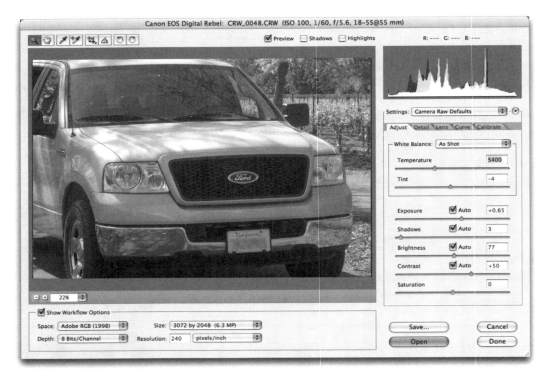

❶ Click File>Open.

❷ Navigate to the CRW file, select it and click Open.

❸ Photoshop's Camera Raw dialog box opens in Basic Mode.

- A preview of the image is displayed.

- The photo's ISO, shutter speed, F-stop, and lens information are displayed at the top of the dialog.

- From the Adjust tab you can make white balance, exposure, shadows, brightness, contrast, and saturation adjustments.

- The Detail tab allows you to adjust sharpness, luminance smoothing, and color noise reduction.

❹ Advanced Mode offers Lens and Calibrate options as well.

Save That RAW Setting

If you're importing many photos from the same session, you can save the settings you make to the first and apply them to other photos.

1. Open a CRW image and make the necessary adjustments.
2. Select Save Settings... from the sub menu.
3. Save with a descriptive name.
4. Click OK to open the photo.
5. Open another CRW file.
6. In the Settings box, select the setting you created.
7. The preview image is adjusted.
8. Click OK.

Caught in the Web

Your client may refer you to their web page for images to use on television. Resist this at all costs! Formats like JPEG, GIF, and PNG are highly compressed formats designed for quick display over the Internet, not for TV(though, if forced, PNGs are the least of all web-evils). When these files are created from scratch or from larger, higher-resolution files, data such as color and image detail information are thrown out in the compression stage. GIF files are especially bad since they use a palette of only 256 colors. Most clients just don't understand that you won't get good results from web graphics. If the logo is simple, you may be able to use it as a template and re-create it in Illustrator or Photoshop, but if you don't have the time or expertise to do that, insist on a higher-resolution bitmap—or even better—a vector-based logo.

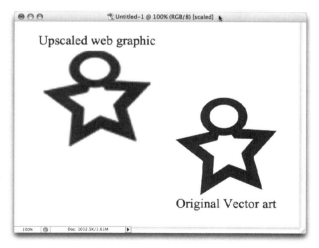

Upscaled web graphic

Original Vector art

Capture the Moment

It's common to use still images captured from video clips in TV graphics. An image from a news story, for example, may look great in an over-the-shoulder slide as the anchor reads the lead.

1 Export a still frame from your non-linear editing system, or look at programs like QuickTime Pro (www.quicktime.com) or Tools For Television Pro (www.toolsfortelevision.com) for frame-grab capability.

2 Open the frame grab in Photoshop.

3 Since your frame grab will likely be a two-field frame, you may see some comb-like distortion, especially in a shot with movement. Not a problem: use the De-Interlace filter to get rid of those comb teeth (Filter>Video>De-Interlace). When you apply the filter, Photoshop asks which fields to eliminate. Select either odd or even (that's entirely up to you) and choose to create the new fields by Interpolation. Photoshop will throw out one set of fields and replace it with a new set, smoothing the image out nicely.

4 If the Image is opened in Photoshop CS, ensure the Pixel Aspect Ratio is being correctly interpreted. Choose Image>Pixel Aspect Ratio>[format you acquired from, i.e. D1/DV NTSC]. If you're using an older version of Photoshop, you may need to resize to the proper square pixel frame size such as 720X540 for NTSC or 768X576 for PAL.

5 Compensate for YUV levels by adjusting the black and white points of the image.

Choose Image>Adjustments>Levels or press Cmd+L (Ctrl+L).

Work with the Input Levels.

Set the Black Point to 16 for Black and set the White Point to 235.

Advice When Scanning

You can get a perfectly acceptable USB powered scanner that is cross-platform for $100. Sure you can spend more and get more, but chances are you scan only a few items per project. Here are a few tips to keep in mind about scanning images.

- The most important thing when scanning is to be consistent. In a multi-user environment, this means posting the scanning guidelines on the scanner lid.

- Ensure that the scanner is lying flat, or you may get misregistered scans.

- Use a gentle glass cleaner whenever smudges appear. Spray the cleaner on the soft cloth, and then wipe the scanner bed down.

- Place your photos on the scanner straight. Use the edges to help you maintain parallel edges on your photos. If you get crooked photos, try Photoshop CS's newest automation tool File>Automate>Crop and Straighten Photos.

- If you are scanning three-dimensional objects place a piece of clear glass or plastic on top of your scanner's tray to protect it from scratches. You can also remove the scanner's lid and place a shadow box or black cloth on top of large objects.

- Save to uncompressed formats such as TIFF, PICT, or TARGA for maximum compatibility and disk space usage. The PSD format is great for layered files, but is not as efficient for single layered files. Always save the appropriate file extension for your file type.

- Routinely check your manufacturer's website for new drivers. This software improves upon how well your scanner interfaces with Photoshop. The updates are generally free.

- If your scanner malfunctions, power down your system, and check your cable connections. When satisfied, power up the scanner first and restart your computer. If the problem is not fixed, check for new drivers.

Image courtesy Himera Photo Objects

ON THE SPOT

CHAPTER 3

Lay It On!
Getting the Most from the Layers Palette

When Photoshop first shipped, it did not have layers. It was an application that worked extremely well for touching up photos, frames of film, or video stills. It was a program with only a few purposes, but a passionate fan base that wanted to see it do more.

The introduction of layers moved Photoshop from image touch-up program to a robust graphics tool. If you want to be fast in Photoshop, you must understand the Layers Palette.

Think of layers as tracks from a video timeline. The way you build and organize the show affects your end results. With proper organization, you can come back later and quickly make changes. Using features like color-coding, layer sets, grouping, and clear naming, make it easier to move the project into After Effects or your nonlinear edit system. Mastering layers is your first step to becoming a Photoshop power user.

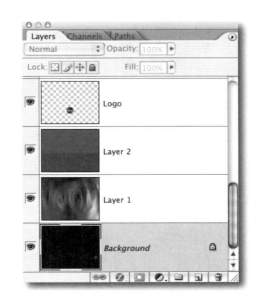

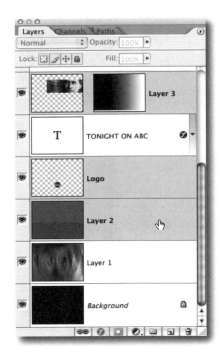

Want to Manipulate More Than One Layer?

Photoshop CS2 now gives us the ability to select more than one layer at a time. Just hold down the Command key (Control) and click on layer names to select multiple layers at a time. Want to select contiguous layers? You can hold down the shift key and select a range of layers. Feel free to change the opacity, free transform, or move the layers around all at once.

Where'd My Linking Column Go?

One of the first things you'll notice about Photoshop CS2 is that it has removed the column for linking layers.

- This is now accomplished by selecting the layers that you want to link and contextual-clicking on one of the selected layers and choosing Link Layers. You can also click the link button at the bottom of the Layers Palette.

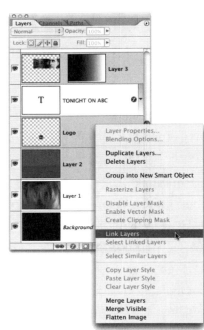

- Unlinking layers is accomplished by selecting all of the linked layers and selecting Unlink Layers from the same menu.

- If you find it takes too long to select all of your linked layers, simply contextual-click on one of your linked layers and choose Select Linked Layers.

Want to "See" How Your Layers Are Linked?
Give Groups a Try

If you don't like linking your layers because it is visually difficult to see what is linked, you can group your layers. Groups are new in CS2 (and we don't mean Group as in clipping mask). Prior versions referred to groups as layer sets.

❶ First, select the layers that you want to group.

❷ Then press Cmd+G (Ctrl+G) to bring the layers into a group.

If you want to remove items from a group, select the group folder in the Layers palette and use Cmd+Shift+G (Ctrl+Shift+G) to bring them out of the group.

Or, if you have time to kill (yeah... right) you can click the group button at the bottom of the Layers palette to create the group and then drag each layer into it one at a time.

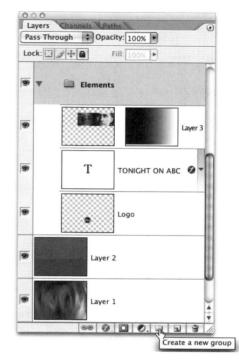

Lost in a Sea of Layers

If you find yourself lost in the Layers palette trying to find the exact layer you are looking for, maybe you need to organize them. The easiest way is to organize layers is by combining them into a Smart Object. This new feature in Photoshop CS2 joins your layers into a single layer called a Smart Object.

This is essentially a file nested in a layer (much like pre-composing inside of After Effects).

When you double click on the Smart Object, a new window opens in Photoshop that contains all of the original layers that were used to create the Smart Object. Changes can be made to each layer within the Smart Object, and when saved, the changes are reflected in the document that contains the Smart Object. Very cool idea Adobe!

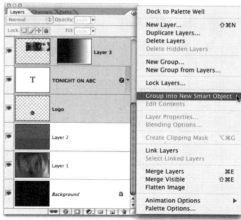

Locking Things Down

How many times have you shared your Photoshop files with someone that you are collaborating with only to have them returned with layers out of position, or finished layers painted over? If you haven't, you're lucky (or the only graphic artist on staff).

At the top of the Layers palette there is an area that allows you to lock the attributes of each layer.

❶ Select the layer that you want to lock.

❷ Select the locking option that meets your needs.

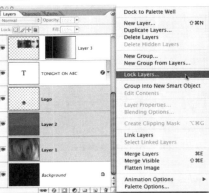

- The first box locks the transparent pixels for that layer and keeps you (or someone else) from filling or painting over transparent areas of the layer.

- The second box locks the image pixels so that you cannot delete or paint over existing pixels in the layer.

- The third box locks the position of the layer so that you cannot re-position the contents of the layer.

- The fourth box locks it all down so that you cannot make any changes to the pixels, transparency or position of the contents of the layer.

The good news? You can combine combinations of locking techniques by clicking on multiple buttons. To unlock a property, just click its button a second time.

Sure, You Can Lock More Than One Layer at a Time

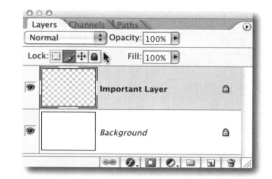

Locking is great... so great you might start locking things all the time! There are two fast and easy ways to lock more than one layer at a time.

First, you can place all of the items that you wish to lock into a group. Then select Lock All Layers in Group from the Layer Palette menu. This will apply the same lock to all of the layers within that group. NOTE: If you try to lock the group itself, you will only protect the group. If you try to individually manipulate the layers within the group, you will still be able to modify them.

The second way to lock multiple layers is to select the layers that you want to lock, then select Lock Layers from the Layers menu. This will bring up a dialog that will let you choose the attributes that you wish to lock.

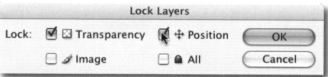

Smart Objects Part Deux

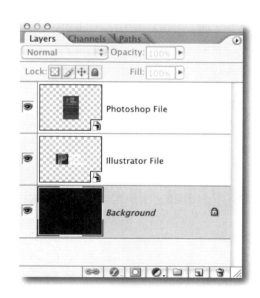

In previous versions of Photoshop, the Place function under the File menu only allowed you to place vector based files such as EPS and Illustrator files in your Photoshop document. Now with Smart Objects, you can place other Photoshop files in your current file as a Smart Object.

- Keep in mind that Photoshop now places a copy of your Photoshop file in the Smart Object, and becomes its own entity.

- Making changes to the original file placed object outside of the new document does not change or update the Smart Object.

- However, you can replace the content of a Smart Object by replacing it with the original changed file. Do this by selecting the Smart Object layer, and use Replace Content under the Layer, Smart Object menu.

Send Your Smart Objects off to College

So we've got you convinced that Smart Objects are the way to go. The good news is you can also export Smart Object layers as individual Photoshop files for you to work with. Just choose Layer>Smart Object>Export Contents.

Looks Great Together, but What About by Itself

Ever want to look at a layer all by itself, but didn't want to go through and turn all of the other layers invisible? In a video edit, this is often called soloing a track... well Photoshop can do it too!

- Simply Option+click (Alt+click) on the eyeball icon for the layer that you want to view and all of the other layers' visibility will be turned off.

- Want to go back to the visibility state you were just in? No problem (remember this is Photoshop you are working with!) Simply Option+click (Alt+click) click on the layer's eyeball again and everything that was visible when you started is back on again.

To Overlay or Lighten, That Is the Question

Blend modes are the best thing since sliced bread in your creative toolbox (hopefully you don't have sliced bread in your toolbox!) But don't you just hate grabbing the blend mode menu and selecting them one at a time? Us too.

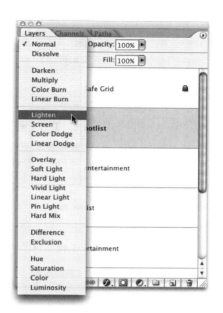

❶ Choose a tool like Move or Marquee (the key is a tool that doesn't have its own blend modes like a paint brush)

❷ Then select the layer you want to modify its blend mode.

❸ Press Shift+= (equals) to move down the list one at a time, or Shift+- (minus) to move up the list one at a time.

It All Comes Down to Resolution

Whenever you are working in Photoshop, the key to success is leaving yourself room for error. The ability to make changes is key to your success. One of the best rules you can follow is to always work with tools and create layers that are based on vector artwork. Examples of these would be text layers and shape layers. Because these layer types are resolution independent, you can resize, scale, transform and manipulate infinitely without degrading the resolution.

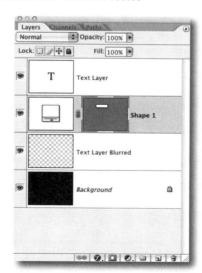

So the next time you need to draw a box, a circle or any other shape, use the shape tool with its options set to shape layers or paths, NOT a filled region. And if you need to render a text layer to apply a filter to it, always copy your text layer before applying the filter so you can go back and make changes to the text if you need to later. Future proofing ensures you won't miss a deadline!

I Need a New Layer and I Need It NOW!

You can quickly create new layers without letting your fingers leave your keyboard. Here are the three most popular Layers palette keyboard shortcuts.

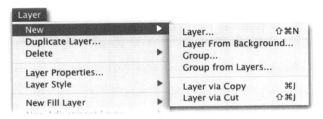

- Command+Shift+N (Control+Shift+N) will create a new empty layer above your current layer.

- Command+J (Control+J) will create a new layer by copying the selected area on your current layer and placing it on a new layer.

- Command+Shift+J (Control+Shift+J) will create a new layer by cutting the selected area on your current layer and placing it on a new layer.

- Ok, one more for the road. If you hold down the Command (Control) key while clicking the new layer button at the bottom of the Layer's palette, you will create a new layer below your current layer.

The Difference Between Opacity and Fill

At the top of the Layers palette you will notice two adjustment boxes, one for the opacity and one for the fill for a layer. At first glance, they seem to do the same thing, but they are very different.

- The opacity slide will adjust the opacity of the entire layer, content and layer styles such as drop shadows.

- If you adjust the fill, you are only adjusting the opacity of the layer content, but the opacity of your layer styles are left unaffected. Using a drop shadow or bevel and emboss style with the fill set to zero allows for a variety of text effects that leave your text completely editable.

Need to Erase the Background From a Photo, but Don't Want to Lose It Forever?

Pros don't waste their time with the Magic Eraser or the Extract Command. Instead they turn to layer masks, which give you ultimate control over removing elements from an image (plus they maintain the ability to get content back again).

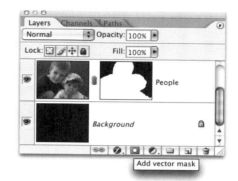

❶ You create a layer mask by clicking Add Layer Mask at the bottom of the Layer palette. If you have a selection before clicking the button, Photoshop will use this and add an initial mask.

❷ With the layer mask selected (look for a border around the right thumbnail), you can use the brush tool to paint black into the layer you paint; you will see your image disappear.

❸ The good news is, if you want something back, switch to white and paint it back in. A very useful set of keyboard shortcuts can be learned by the pneumonic devil's xylophone. D loads the default colors of black and white, X toggles between those colors.

There is really no reason to destructively edit your layers with this powerful technique. You can take this a step further by unlocking the mask from the layer content and positioning the mask independent of the image to place it exactly where you want it.

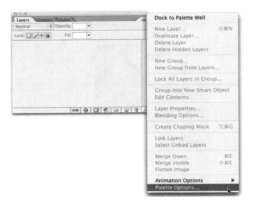

It's All in the Options

The Layers palette can be customized to look and work the way you like it best. By default, Photoshop sets the Layers palette icon to a small icon but you've got options.

Access the controls through the palette's submenu by selecting Palette Options.

- You can select from three icon sizes or turn them them off altogether.

- Change their bounds and content of the thumbnails

- Change how adjustment layer masks are handled.

Are You in Style?

Using layer styles brings life to your layers. These are accessed at the bottom of the Layer palette and give you the ability to add a variety of different effects to your images from drop shadows to outlines and glows, to bevels, colorizations and textures.

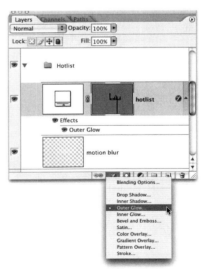

- You can add as many as you want to a layer to combine effects.

- You can turn them on and off by contextual-clicking on the layer style icon on the layer and selecting Disable or Enable Layer Effects.

- This menu also gives you feedback on the styles that are currently used. By selecting one from the menu, the dialog for that style is opened.

Leftovers Anyone?

If you create a look or overall style that you like on a given layer, you can save it for later.

❶ With the layer selected that you want to save the style for, select Styles from the Window menu to open the Styles palette.

❷ Click the New Style button at the bottom of the palette and your style will be saved for later enjoyment.

❸ When you are ready to use it again, pick the layer that you want to apply it to, and click on the style you created in the Style palette. All of your style settings are 'reheated' and an applied to the layer.

Don't Hurt Your Layers, Help Them Adjust

We've never met a producer or client who didn't like to make changes (last-minute ones at that!). Well Photoshop has got you covered. Adjustment layers are a very powerful, non-destructive way to correct image problems on your layers. Just click on the black and white circle at the bottom of the Layers palette. Here you will find Levels, Curves, Color Balance, Brightness/Contrast, plus a slew of other ways to adjust the appearance of a layer. The best part is that they don't permanently change the content of your layer, and can be fine tuned, stacked or even turned off. If you find your self making exposure or color adjustments to your layers, do yourself a favor and do it with an adjustment layer. You will save hours of time in the long run.

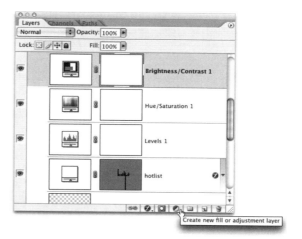

43

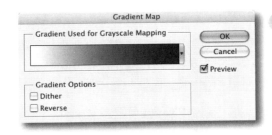

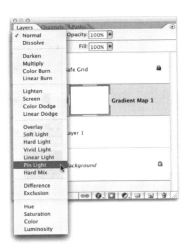

Did You Say NTSC Colors in the Layers Palette?

Well, to be honest, no we didn't. But this is a killer technique that will allow you to deal with oversaturated colors in images that run the risk of bleeding on video.

❶ Apply a Gradient Map adjustment layer to the top of your image.

❷ Choose the black to white gradient from the default gradient menu that appears. If necessary, choose to reload the default gradient set.

❸ Apply the Pin Light transfer mode to the adjustment layer and voila! Instant color taming for potentially dangerous oversaturated colors.

Who Needs Clippings Masks?

Aren't clipping masks for print designers? Well, yes but what's good for the goose is also good for the gander. Clipping masks are a very fast and easy way to create an image on text effect. Clipping masks take a layer and make them only visible on the opaque areas of the layer below them.

❶ For example, create a text or shape layer.

❷ Place a digital photo above it.

❸ With the photo layer selected, choose Create Clipping Mask from the Layer menu.

Notice how the photo is cut into the shape of the text or shape layer? The best news here is that you can import this Photoshop file right into After Effects and it will keep your clipping mask effect intact and ready for animating. Apply an Outer Glow Layer Style to the text and it looks even snazzier! Eat your heart out goose!

What's a Chapter on Layers Without Mentioning Merge?

Had you worried for a moment didn't we? Here's a simple yet useful tip. Ever need to quickly create a layer at the top of your image that is a composite of all the visible layers below it, but don't want to merge because it will destroy your layer integrity? Well the option (alt) key just became your best friend.

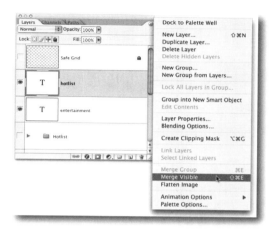

❶ Create a new layer at the top of your image.

❷ Holding down the option (Alt) key.

❸ Choose Merge Visible from the Layers palette sub-menu.

The result is a composite of all visible layers in the newly created layer, without loosing your layers below. Of course leave out the option/alt key and all your visible layers get merged into the currently selected layer (probably a bad idea). This is a great way to create a layer to load as a selection for creating your alpha channels.

My Eyes Are Good, but Not That Good

So you are working on a lower third and you want to make sure that the logo on top of the text bar is in the exact vertical center of the bar. Easy, let Photoshop do it for you.

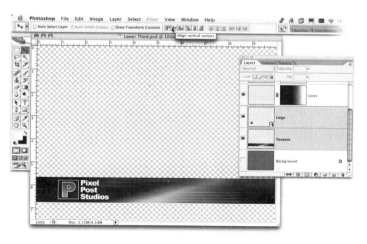

❶ Using the Command (Control) key, select the two layers that you want to align.

❷ Select the Move tool (v).

❸ Click Align vertical centers from the move tool options palette.

That does it. The two layers are not aligned vertically. There are also options for aligning horizontal centers, as well as top, bottom, left and right edges. Any layers that are selected when you do an alignment will be factored into the move (except for the Background layer and layers that have their position locked.

Sexy Factoids!

Time for a real world example. You are making a full screen factoid graphic. You designed this killer icon to act as the bullet marker for each item. You spread the icons out, but you can't tell if they are evenly spaced. Again, Photoshop to the rescue.

❶ Select all of the icon layers using the Command (Control) key and clicking on the layers.

❷ Select the Move tool (V).

❸ Click the Distribute top edges option for the move tool.

And yet again, Photoshop has worked magic that mere mortals can only dream of!

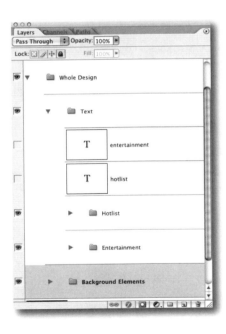

That Was So Good, May I Have More Please!

So now that you have seen layer groups, you just can't get enough. Good news, you can create as many as you want in the same document, and better yet you can place Layer Groups inside other Layer Groups. Name them, stack them, and nest them. Now you have more computing power to manipulate your images than the first men who traveled to the moon.

Did You Forget to Bring Your Highlighter?

No problem, Photoshop has got you covered. Now we are taking visual organization to the next level by color-coding your layers. If your text books in high school looked like they lost an ink war, then you will love this feature.

1 Contextual-click on a layer and select Layer Properties.

2 Select a color from the pull down menu labeled Color.

Your layer is now conveniently color labeled. This helps you keep track of important text layers, or other objects that you need to pay close attention to.

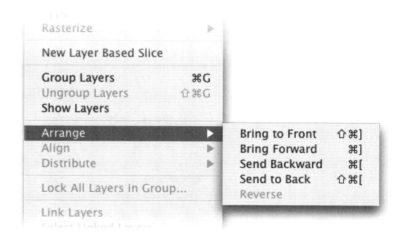

Shuffleboard Anyone?

I know, I don't have time to play shuffleboard either, but you can have just as much fun moving your layers around in the Layer palette. There are two methods you can use for rearranging the order of your layers.

- The simplest is to click on a layer with you mouse and drag it to a new position.

- You can also use keyboard shortcuts to move a layer.

    Move layer up one step: Cmd+] (Cntrl+])

    Move layer down one step: Cmd+[(Cntrl +[)

    Move layer to the top: Cmd+Shift+] (Cntrl+Shift+])

    Move layer to the bottom: Cmd+Shift+[(Cntrl+Shift+[)

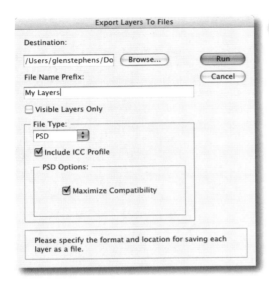

I Love My Layers So Much, I Want a File of Each One.

Photoshop layers are the foundation of working in Photoshop, however not all applications support them. If you want to take your Photoshop image into and editing program as multiple layers, but your NLE doesn't support layered Photoshop files, here is your ticket.

❶ Select File>Scripts>Export Layers as Files.

❷ Dial in your options

❸ Click Run.

It's that simple. Photoshop has just created a single file for each layer in your document and saved it to the location that you specified.

Need Transparency on the Background?

So you're working on your Background and you need some transparency... you make a selection on the Background layer and hit delete... only to see fill it with the Background color? What gives? If you are trying to create transparent areas on the Background layer, you will need to turn the Background layer into a standard layer.

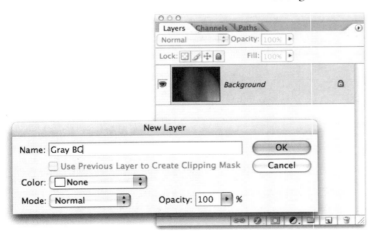

❶ Double click on the Background layer in the Layers palette

❷ Rename it to the default name, "Layer 0", or any other name that makes you a happier designer.

Now as a standard layer, you can delete pixels and create transparency to your heart's content.

Choices, Choices and More Choices.

Options are what it's all about. Your success as a designer will be greatly tied to your ability to give your client options. When you are working on a new design for a show, your client wants to see variations of the image. This is where Layer Comps come in extremely handy. Layer Comps (Window>Layer Comps). You can make changes to your document and let Layer Comps remember the states of your image. There are 3 things that Layer Comps will remember.

- Layer Position

- Layer Visibility

- Appearance, or Layer Style.

Here is how you use them.

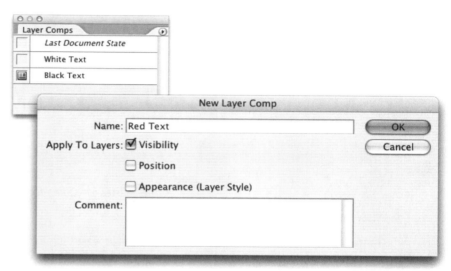

❶ Open the Layer Comp palette.

❷ Create a new Layer Comp.

❸ Choose the attributes that you want this comp to remember.

❹ Change your layers position, layer visibility, and styles to create a new variation of the image.

❺ Create a new Layer Comp.

You can now toggle back and forth between the comps to see the different states of the image. Layer comps don't remember fonts for text layers or the color of pixel on a layer. Therefore we recommend using layer styles to color your layers, and not actually fill the pixels. This adds much more flexibility to your comps. When you have your variations saved as Layer Comps, use the File>Scripts>Layer Comps to Files to save each comp as its own psd or pdf that you can send to your client for approval.

ON THE SPOT

Channel Operations

Gaining Control Over Images Through the Channels Palette

Every Photoshop image has at least one channel that carries color information. RGB images, which are commonly used for video, have three channels: one each for the red, green, and blue color information. You can also add an alpha channel to an image, which works as a matte, determining which pixels in the image are transparent and which pixels are opaque.

Channels work much the same way as layers, and by default the Channels palette is docked with the Layers palette. If you don't see your Layers palette, select Window>Layers to open it. Color channels give you incredible power in editing images and can be of tremendous help in making selections. Let's see how.

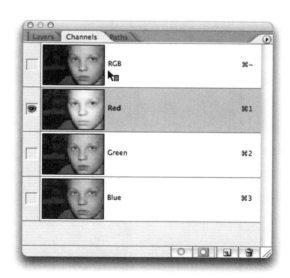

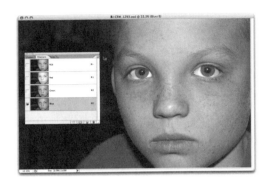

Color Me Gray

RGB images carry three separate channels: one each for the red, green, and blue color information. When you edit an RGB image you normally see the composite of these three channels. However, Photoshop automatically separates the colors and represents each channel with a grayscale image in the Channels Palette. An image contains the most amount of a given color where that color channel's grayscale image is lightest. Conversely, the composite image contains the least amount of a given color where that color channel's grayscale image is darkest, or black. Read channels like you read masks. Black represents minimum saturation and white represents maximum saturation.

See What You Can See

Another important kind of channel is the alpha channel. Instead of color information, alpha channels define transparency. Photoshop represents alpha channels with grayscale images, too. When the channel's grayscale image is black you can effectively block that data from showing through in your nonlinear editor. Where the grayscale image is white, you will see the pixel data at its highest level of opacity.

Alpha channels are also useful for saving selections. An RGB image can carry more than 50 alpha channels. This can be useful in storing selections for later use, but most NLEs have trouble reading multiple alpha channels. When saving for import into a video application, be sure to delete any inactive alpha channels.

Selections

Alpha channels are often based on selections. An intricate selection is rarely made in one fell swoop. Many people waste precious time trying to outline a detailed section of an image with the lasso tool in one shot. A better idea is to use a series of quick, small selections using a variety of selection tools. Hold Shift to add to the current selection and Option (Alt) to subtract from it. This method makes for the most useful and accurate selections. Here are some tips:

- Use both the Rectangular and Elliptical Marquee tools to create small selections that build on one another.

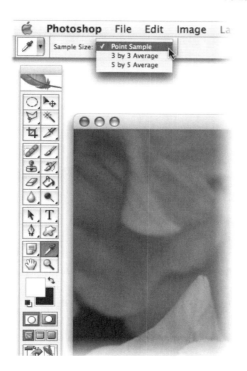

- When using Marquee tools, press the spacebar to move your selection around the image and the Shift key to constrain the selection's proportions.

- The Magic Wand tool uses the settings in the Eyedropper Tool. Select the Eyedropper Tool and set the Sample Size to 3x3 Average or 5x5 Average instead of Point Sample. See how that changes your selections with the Magic Wand tool.

- When using the Lasso tools, switch between the Polygonal Lasso Tool and the Lasso Tool by holding the Option (Alt) key while dragging.

Quick – Gimme a Mask

Quick Mask mode allows you to manipulate your selection as if it was a mask. This is an incredibly easy and versatile way to add to and subtract from selections. Let's assume you want to start with a rough selection.

1 Make a rough selection in your image.

2 Click the Edit in Quick Mask Mode button near the bottom of the toolbox or press the keyboard shortcut Q to enter Quick Mask mode.

3 Selected areas are displayed normally; unselected areas are displayed with a color overlay.

4 Using the Brush Tool, paint white to add to the selection. This erases the color overlay.

5 If you make a mistake, you can simply paint black to subtract from the selection.

6 Press Q to leave Quick Mask mode.

7 Your modified selection appears.

Set It Straight

There are two kinds of alpha channels: premultiplied and straight. When an alpha channel with soft edges is created over a background, some of the background color is composited with the alpha channel. This creates an alpha channel that has been premultiplied with another color. Some of these background-colored pixels will show up as nasty soft fringe when you try to composite the image over a different-colored background. To avoid this, adjust your image's background image to match the color of your shadow or glow.

Quick Notes on Quick Masks

- Before you enter Quick Mask mode, press the keyboard shortcut D to return to the default foreground and background colors of black and white.

- Quickly switch between the foreground and background colors by pressing the keyboard shortcut X.

- You can go in and out of Quick Mask mode as much as you want.

- Softer brushes create feathered selections.

- The Brush, Smudge and Blur tools all work on Quick Masks.

- When you enter Quick Mask mode "(Quick Mask)" appears in the title bar of your document and a new channel called Quick Mask appears in the Channels Palette.

- You cannot directly save your quick mask as a channel. To turn the Quick Mask into an alpha channel, leave Quick Mask mode and click the Save Selection as Channel button in the Channels Palette.

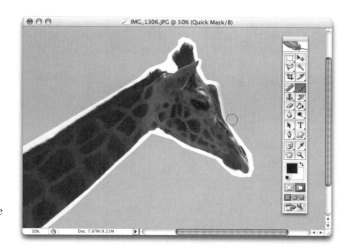

To See or Not to See...

Defining transparency in your images is simple—it literally takes a few seconds to create an alpha channel. Let's assume you want to make a selection first, then create an alpha channel based on that selection.

1 Make a selection using any selection tool.

2 In the Channels Palette click "Save Selection as Channel."

3 A new channel called Alpha 1 appears in the palette.

4 Click the visibility icon next to the alpha channel.

5 By default, masked pixels appear with a 50% rubylith overlay.

Change the Channel

Chances are the new alpha channel won't be exactly what you need. Don't worry, you can edit your new alpha channel to perfection. There are a few different ways to view the alpha channel while you clean it up. The first is to work with the color overlay with the image behind it.

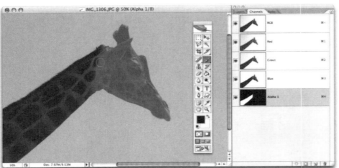

1 Press the keyboard shortcut D to bring up the default colors of black and white.

2 Click the alpha channel's icon in the Channels Palette. The channel is highlighted. The overlay appears over masked areas.

3 Paint black to mask pixels and white to show pixels.

4 Click the visibility indicator to turn the overlay off when you're done.

Seeing Gray

Photoshop also allows you to see just the grayscale alpha channel without the image behind it.

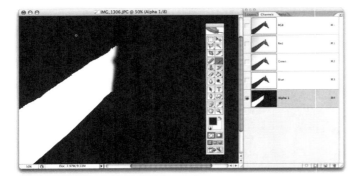

1 Turn the Alpha Channel's visibility off by clicking the eye icon next to it in the Channels Palette

2 Click the RGB channel of the image to highlight the color channels

3 Holding Option (Alt), click the alpha channel's icon

4 The alpha channel appears. Make necessary adjustments using the Brush,Smudge.

5 Click the visibility indicator next to the RGB channel to see the image again.

Notes on Alpha Channels

- Change the color and the designation of the overlay by double clicking the alpha channel icon. The Channel Options dialog appears. Here you can rename the channel, choose whether the overlay appears on masked or selected pixels, and even choose a different overlay color.

- Since alpha channels are pixel-based, you can run filters on them. Try adding a Blur filter to soften edges.

- RGB images can carry up to 53 alpha channels. Keep in mind when you import an image to an NLE it will probably only read one alpha channel correctly.

- Alpha channels can have soft edges and gradient transparencies.

- Use the Levels command (Image>Adjustments> Levels) to adjust the contrast in the alpha channel.

- Drag an alpha channel to the Channels palette's trash can icon to delete it.

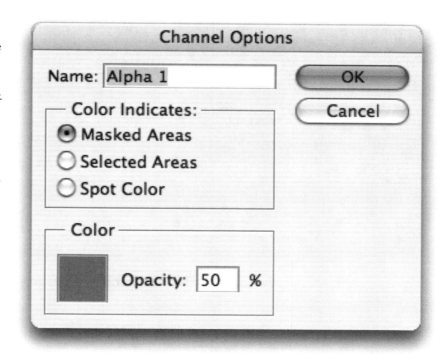

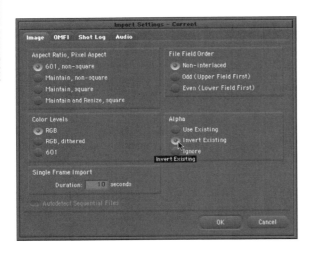

Avid Users Fear Not

Because of their film origins, Avid systems read alpha channels backward from Photoshop and just about every nonlinear editing system. The call this a "film" alpha and it means that the areas you define as masked in Photoshop will show through in Avid systems, and those you want to show through will be hidden. If you use Avid exclusively, you can just get used to using alpha channels the opposite way, but if you work with many different applications it can be annoying. Good thing there's an easy fix.

1 Create and save your graphic with its alpha channel as usual.

2 Import to Avid, navigate to the file and select Options.

3 In the Alpha box click Invert Existing.

4 Click Open to import the file.

5 Avid will retain this setting until you change it.

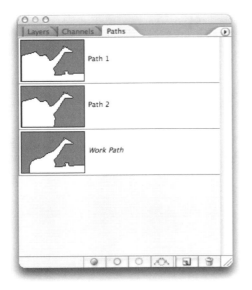

The Path to Serving Selections...

So you spent several minutes making a detailed selection, then the client has a change of heart. So you spend several more minutes making another selection, and the client discovers he or she liked the first idea better. It's a good idea to save detailed selections as paths if you think you might need them later.

1 With your selection active, switch to the Paths palette.

2 Click the Make Work Path From Selection button at the bottom of the palette.

3 Double click the new path to rename it.

4 To delete a path, drag it to the trash can or choose Paths>Delete Path.

5 To load a selection based on a path, Cmd+click (Ctrl+click) the path.

If you don't rename each path, the next one you make will replace it. Paths can be saved with any document created with a Mac. Windows users can save paths in PSD, JPEG, JPEG 2000, DCS, EPS, PDF, and TIFF formats. Please note, Paths do not support feathered edges or gradients.

Look No Further

Sometimes one of your color channels will look a lot like what you want your alpha channel to look like. Since color channels and alpha channels are both defined by grayscale images, wouldn't it be cool if you could create an alpha channel based on a color channel? Well, you can-and what's better is that you can even combine information from more than one color channel to create an alpha channel. Increase the size of the channel thumbnails to get a better look at the grayscale images by Ctrl+clicking (right-clicking) anywhere in the Channels Palette.

To create a new alpha channel from a single color channel:

1 Cmd+click (Ctrl+click) on the color channel's icon to load that channel as a selection.

2 Click Save Selection as Channel from the bottom of the Channels palette.

3 A new channel labeled Alpha 1 appears.

4 Turn the new channel's visibility on to see the overlay of the new alpha channel on your image.

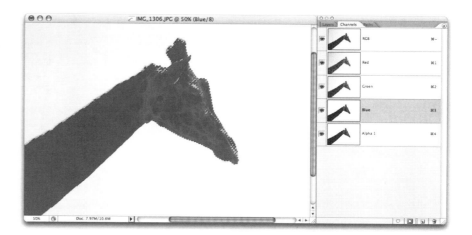

According to My Calculations...

A single color channel will create a perfect alpha in some images, but for the most part you'll get a better selection by combining color channels.

To create a new alpha channel from more than one color channel:

1 Click on the channel with the highest contrast to select it.

2 Select Image>Calculations.

3 A dialog box appears. This allows you to combine color channels and make the composite grayscale image a new channel, selection, or document.

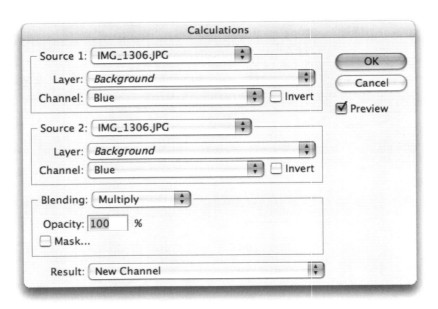

4 The channel you selected appears as source one. Select the second highest contrast image for source two.

5 Make sure Preview is enabled.

6 Scroll through the blend modes to create the highest possible contrasting image. Also try inverting source two by clicking the Invert option.

7 When you get a high contrast image, make sure New Channel is selected in the Result box and click OK.

8 Your new alpha channel appears in the Channels Palette.

Remember, the goal is to get a good mask for your particular image. If that means completely masking lots of pixels, try to create a black and white image, or something close to it. If that means a gradual masking of pixels, shoot for more of a grayscale image. Remember, you can always use a Levels adjustment on the new Alpha channel to refine it.

Strut Your Style

Adding drop shadow, bevel and glow effects to your layers can quickly spice them up. However, these layer effects aren't included in the selection that loads when you Cmd+click (Ctrl+click) a layer's icon. For example, when you add a drop shadow to vector text, then Ctrl+click the layer to load the selection, you'll notice the drop shadow is outside the selection. This can really be a pain when you try to create an alpha channel based on a selection. The alpha channel masks the layer style. Here's a solution:

1 Create a new document with a transparent background.

2 Using the Type tool, create a few lines of text.

3 Double click the text layer to bring up the Layer Style dialog and add a drop shadow and a bevel to the text .

4 Create a new layer by clicking the Create a New Layer button at the bottom of the Layers palette.

5 Link the layers by clicking the Link button (next to the Visibility icon) on the layer that is not active.

6 With the new layer still selected, hold Option (Alt) and select Merge Linked from the Layers Palette submenu.

7 The type, complete with the drop shadow and bevel layer effects, is rasterized on the new layer.

8 Turn the original text layer's visibility off.

9 Cmd+click (Ctrl+click) the new layer to load the selection.

10 Switch to the Channels palette and click Save Selection as Channel to create an alpha channel that won't mask the layer effects.

With this method, you cannot edit the text once you merge to the new layer. If you need to make a change, delete the rasterized layer, edit the original text layer and repeat steps 4-10.

ON THE SPOT

CHAPTER 5

Background Check
Still and Motion Backgrounds for the TV Screen

In case you're overworked and tired, we wanted to remind you that your world is much more complex than those who work in print. You see (literally), unlike these words on this page, which are easy to read over a plain white background, you just can't get away with that in video.

The use of backgrounds, whether static or dynamic is essential to good broadcat design. In this chapter, we'll tackle creating some great backdrops for your broadcast and motion graphics. We'll use both Photoshop and After Effects to create this important "wallpaper."

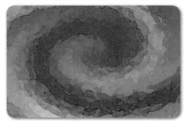

It's Not Laziness, It's Efficiency!

This chapter will cover a lot of design techniques for creating your own backgrounds in Photoshop and After Effects, but when you just need a slam dunk solution that is quick and efficient, there are hundreds of stock libraries available for video designers that come with ready-made static and motion backgrounds. Here are a few resources that you will find useful for stock backgrounds.

- Animation Factory – www.animationfactory.com/video
- Artbeats – www.artbeats.com
- Atomic Fuel – www.atomic-fuel.com
- Digital Juice – www.digitaljuice.com
- TDM Stock – www.tastedigitalmedia.com
- Tools for Television Photoshop Toolbox – www.toolsfortelevision.com

I Think I Can, I Think I Can

Don't think that creating your own background is difficult. Here is the easiest way to quickly create your own custom background.

1. Open up any image or digital photo that has a high contrast range to it or a variety of colors.

2. Apply a 45° Motion Blur (Filter>Blur>Motion Blur) with the Distance setting all the way up.

3. If the lines that are created are too defined, use a Gaussian Blur (Filter>Blur>Gaussian) to soften the effect.

It is that simple. The limiting factor here is that you are locked into the colors of the original photo.

Didn't Black & White Go Out in the 50s?

Well, technically yes, but in Photoshop it is perfect for custom backgrounds. When creating custom backgrounds, we prefer to work with grayscale backgrounds. This allows you to use a colorizing technique that will make it simple to update the color theme of your images very quickly. Here is how to give yourself the flexibility of re-coloring your backgrounds.

❶ Start with a pre-made background or create your own. If it is not grayscale, use Image>Adjustments>Desaturate to strip out the color.

❷ Create a new layer on top of the grayscale background texture.

❸ Change its blend mode to Color.

❹ Now you can fill this layer with a solid color, a gradient with your client's corporate colors, or simply paint color variations onto this layer. The color attributes on this layer will transfer to the grayscale background below.

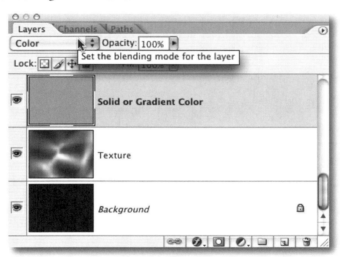

Now when your client decides to change the corporate image in the middle of your production, you are covered.

Logos That Pop!

Your client's logo is their identity. Even though you don't want it to detract from the information within your graphics, you do want it to stand out. Here are some tips for logo treatments that help them stand off the page without slapping you in the face.

- When including them in lower-thirds, use glows, drop shadows, or strokes to separate them from the background.

- If the logo has distinctive lines, or shapes, incorporate similar lines and shapes into the overall design of the background. In a nutshell, don't just plop the logo on top of the background, instead design around its shape and lines.

- Oversize the logo and use a blend mode to blend it in as part of the overall background texture.

- Don't try to use the entire logo in lower-thirds, instead pick a distinguishing feature of the logo and display or incorporate it. This technique creates a theme without using the "bland" slap on the logo type of look. (I would run this one by the client before you implement it.)

A Milkshake Isn't a Milkshake if it's Not Blended...

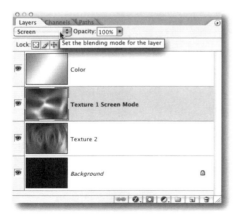

...And neither is a background. Blend modes are your best friend when it comes to creating stylish and eye-catching backgrounds. Layering multiple images and mixing them with blend modes can create incredible effects. It also easily creates originality to your backgrounds so you don't see the exact same stock background on other people's projects. Originality is important for branding, so when you design backgrounds for use in your projects, by simply taking stock backgrounds and combining them with blend modes, you can create something unique very quickly.

Mask It and They Will Come!

Another very effective technique you can use when creating backgrounds for your broadcast graphics is to use layer masks to fade elements in and out of each other. A visually catchy background is usually one that is a composite of various elements that gently fade in and out creating a flowing composition. Here are the steps to down and dirty image comps.

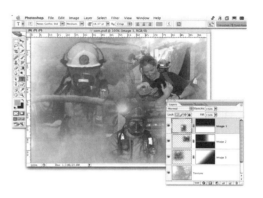

1 Use the marquee tool to grab 3 or 4 elements from different images. Make sure you feather your selections, and grab more than you will need!

2 Once they are all on the same document on their own layers, apply a layer mask to each element.

3 Use a black to white gradient tool and apply gradients to the layer masks for each layer. Experiment with the placement of the gradient to achieve a composite of different images that naturally flows from one element into another.

0 to 60 in 6.8 Seconds

So this creative unique looking stuff is good and all, but I need a slam-dunk lower third and I need it now. Great, here it is in 10 seconds or less.

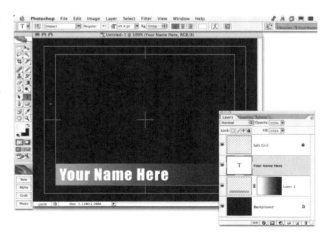

1 Pick your favorite color and put it in the Foreground Color.

2 Use the marquee tool to draw a rectangle inside the title safe area from the left to the right.

3 Create a new empty layer and fill the selection with the foreground color using Option-delete (Alt-delete).

4 Create a layer mask on the layer.

5 Use the black to white gradient tool and draw a gradient on the layer mask from the right edge to the left.

6 Add some text.

Break Out of the Box and Add Some Shapes!

Here is a great way to add a unique quality to your backgrounds. Use the shape tools that Photoshop provides to create backgrounds that aren't all square. There are two tools that you can use to create custom shapes that add style to your backgrounds.

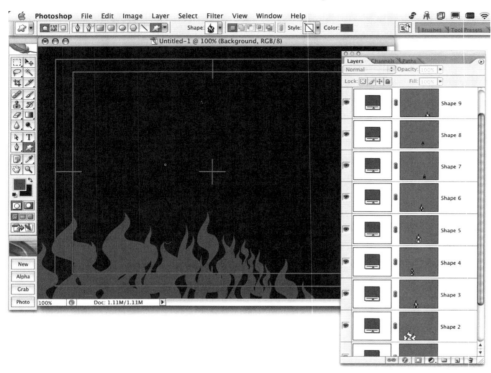

❶ The Shape tools can come in very handy. At first glance, there doesn't appear to be anything useful in there for backgrounds, but by oversizing one of the shapes, duplicating it and offsetting the shapes from each other you can quickly create a unique lower third background.

❷ The pen tool is the king of all tools for creating custom shapes. Use the pen tool to add arcs, curves, or other unique shapes over your square canvas.

Regardless of how you create the shapes, experiment with them and try using them by themselves, or by combining them with more standard rectangular shaped backgrounds.

Who Is That Man Behind the Curtain?

Just because you are creating backgrounds doesn't mean that you need to hide the video behind them. A very appealing technique to creating backgrounds is to use partial backgrounds that do not completely cover the screen, but instead sit on top of a video clip. Also experiment with backgrounds that have a partially transparent alpha channel so that you see the movement of video behind the background. This is a quick tip for creating a semitransparent background.

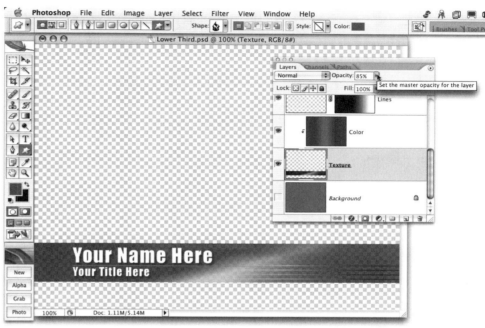

❶ Once you have created a background that you like, make all of the layers that create the background visible.

❷ Merge them onto one layer by selecting Layer>Merge Visible. Make sure that you select a layer other than the background as your merge layer.

❸ Set the transparency of this merged layer to 75% (or whatever value works for your situation).

❹ You can now build the other text or graphic elements on top of this transparent background. When you create an alpha channel for this or take it into your NLE, you can place this over moving video. The background will have a transparent quality while the text and images are opaque on top.

Time to Get Things Moving

Motion backgrounds are not only professional looking, but popular. After Effects is the primary tool that you will use to create motion backgrounds, but the free tool that ships with Photoshop, ImageReady, can also provide you with a quick and easy way to set your backgrounds in motion. In this tip let's take a look at simple ImageReady animation.

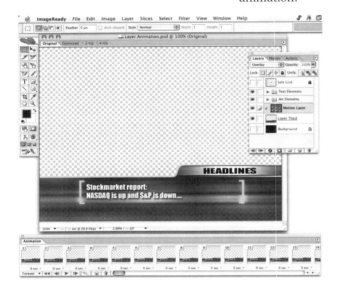

1 Create a background in Photoshop with two full screen backgrounds on separate layers.

2 Apply a blend mode of your choice to the top background element.

3 Move the document to ImageReady by clicking the ImageReady Button at the bottom of the Tool palette.

4 Open the Animation palette under Window>Animation

5 Here we are only going to animate the movement on the blended layer on top. Therefore, move the top layer to its starting position. This is your first keyframe.

6 Create a new animation frame in the Animation palette, and move the layer to its ending position.

7 Select the two animation layers and click the Tween animation button at the bottom of the Animation palette.

8 Enter a value based on frames per second (ie, enter 60 for a two-second animation.) Also, select the position parameter.

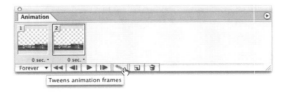

9 Export the animation frames as files (File>Export>Animation frames as files). This provides you with a file per frame of your animation. You can now use QuickTime Pro to create a movie file from the image sequence (File>Open Image Sequence...) and import this into your NLE.

Using After Effects to Animate Your Backgrounds

After Effects provides for an enormous amount of control over creating motion backgrounds. Remember when in Photoshop to keep your elements on separate layers, otherwise you can't move them independently.

1 The key to successfully creating motion backgrounds is to work with images that are larger than a video canvas. Otherwise you will always see the edges of the moving layers. Create a background in Photoshop that is at least twice the size of a video canvas (1440x972.)

2 Import your Photoshop background as a Composition into After Effects (File>Import>File). Be sure to import the file as a Composition, not as footage.

3 You now have a composition with your background elements. So how should you animate your elements? These are the 3 best attributes to animate in After Effects.

- Position

- Size

- Opacity

4 Most of the time, the bottom layer of the comp will not move, but instead you will animate the layers above. Begin creating keyframes for the upper elements to move, scale, and change the opacity for the given elements.

This is the hard part, deciding what to move and at what speed. Take some time to experiment and find a movement that works for the different elements. Here are some tips:

- Start at the beginning of your Timeline and set all of the layer attributes for the start of the animation.

- Move to the end of the Timeline and set all of the layer attributes for the end of the animation.

- Also, try to keep the edges of the elements from getting too close to the middle of the comp.

5 Once you have a motion that works, nest this comp into a comp that is the correct size for your video format.

Shake Things Up a Little Bit

In After Effects (Production Bundle) there is a tool called The Wiggler. This is a very nice tool for creating motion text elements for your titles. This tool is great for youth-oriented programming and upbeat shows.

1 Import your Photoshop title as a composition in After Effects.

2 Create two keyframes for the text element you want to jiggle in the title. They should be Position, Scale, Opacity, or Rotation keyframes. One keyframe should be at the beginning, the other at the end of the timeline. They should be keyframes that are identical—don't make any changes to the start and end keyframes, the effect comes from the keyframes in the middle.

3 Select the two keyframes by holding down the shift key.

4 Open up the Wiggler palette (Window>The Wiggler).

5 Apply the settings that fit the look you are trying to achieve. You can adjust the following parameters:

- Noise type makes the movement either smoother or jagged.

- Dimension controls are for position and scale keyframes and control what dimensions are jiggled, and if they change in the same proportion to each other or not.

- The frequency adjusts how many new keyframes will be created.

- Magnitude controls how big the differences will be from one keyframe to the next.

- The higher the frequency and magnitude numbers are, the more extreme the effect will be.

Looping Background Animations

When creating looping backgrounds, the key is to have the beginning and end keyframes of the animation the same. For example, if your animation uses the position of a layer in After Effects, you want your first and last keyframe for the Position of the layer to be the same X and Y values. The same holds true for all other animated characteristics such as opacity, rotation, or scale. The key is that the movement of everything starts and ends at the same place. When you render motion elements, make sure to render a movie only from the first to the last keyframe. Extra frames rendered at the end beyond the last keyframe will cause the loop to hang.

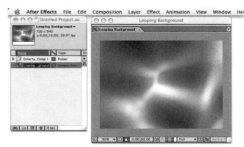

Color Selections

When creating backgrounds for video, remember that they are exactly that, backgrounds. Here are some tips when it comes to color selections for you backgrounds.

- This may seem obvious, but if your client has a color scheme that identifies them, use it in your background designs.

- Use darker, less saturated colors to help the text that is placed on top to stand out and be brighter than the background. Remember the viewer's eye is always first drawn to the brightest element on the screen.

- Remember that colors evoke emotions. Pick colors that evoke the emotional response that you want to achieve from your audience. A great book for color combinations that explain the emotion of color is *Color Harmony: A Guide to Creative Color Combinations* by Hideaki Chijiiwa.

- Avoid over-saturated backgrounds, as they will bleed into the text that sits on top.

- Once you pick a color palette and establish a theme, stick with it throughout all of the graphic elements for that project.

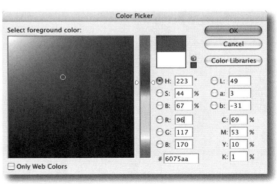

Say It with Words

This is another simple yet commonly overlooked technique. Using text for background elements within your backgrounds is a very effective technique.

- It helps to communicate other subtle messages in your production

- When your creative juices are running dry, text provides great visual elements that can add to the overall design of a background.

- Text creates instant name brand recognition for your client.

You can use single words, a long horizontal string of words separated by bullet points, vertical text elements, or acronyms that correlate to foreground copy. The horizontal and vertical strings of text make great borders or boundary separators for the visual sections of a background.

Using a Letterbox Layout

Another great design tip for creating backgrounds is using a letterbox format as a design element. In Photoshop you can create a letterbox layer over your background, and either change its opacity or blend mode to bring some texture into it. To add an extra special something, create a thin white (or other color) line that sits on top of the edge of the letterbox. Here is how to create the letterbox.

1. Create a new layer at the top of your document.

2. Create a selection the size of your canvas. Cmd-A (Ctrl-A).

3. Next you need to transform the selection. Select>Transform Selection.

4. In the options palette, change the H value to 80%.

5. Hit the enter key to accept the transform command.

6. Invert the selection with Cmd-Shift-I (Ctrl-Shift-I).

7. Fill the selection with black.

Put it in its Place

Even though backgrounds play a secondary role to the content that is sitting on them, you can still use the background to help separate visual elements on the screen. For instance, if you have a title header to your graphic, and content below it, incorporate a visual separator in the background element of your graphic to separate the different content elements. You can create visual separation in your backgrounds with lines, boxes or color changes.

Importing Stock Loops Into After Effects

Did you know that if you want a loop to run longer in After Effects, you don't have to lay the clip into the comp more than once? After Effects has a setting in the Interpret Footage dialog that allows you to set how many times a loop will run for that footage item.

❶ Select the looping element you want to use.

❷ Open the Interpret Footage dialog using Cmd+F (Ctrl+F).

❸ Under Other Options at the bottom of the window you will see a place to specify how many times to loop a given clip. Setting this to 3 for a 10-second loop will now give your footage a duration of 30 seconds.

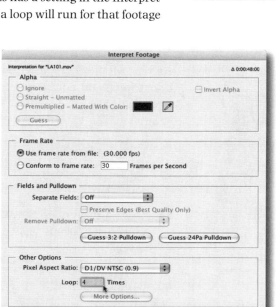

Too Much Contrast

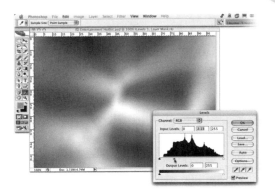

One typical problem that we run into when creating custom backgrounds is that when we are done and place text over them, there is too much contrast and the text gets lost in the textures that we have created. Never fear, Levels are here.

- To tone down the contrast of a given background texture, apply a Levels Adjustment layer above the top layer that makes up your background.

- Under Input levels, you want to adjust the gray point. Moving it to the left will lighten the background, lightening up the dark areas, or moving it to the right will darken the overall background reducing the lighter areas. Usually, we tend to move the gray point to the left to lighten the overall texture.

Animated Backgrounds Don't Always Have to Involve Movement

Another subtle effect you can add to your looping background is a slight change in color through the duration of the loop. In After Effects, this can be accomplished by applying a Hue/Saturation effect to a layer in your comp (Effect>Adjust>Hue Saturation).

1. Check the colorize box.

2. Create your starting and ending keyframes for a given Colorize Hue that fits your theme.

3. Create a keyframe in between the first and last, and offset the Colorize Hue slightly to cause the color to make a subtle adjustment and then return to the original at the end.

You can also animate the saturation and lightness to achieve a similar effect. Using this in combination with other looping techniques really adds a nice look to the finished loop.

Better Safe Than Sorry

We can't finish talking about backgrounds for video than without a quick mention of action and title safe. Obviously, the backgrounds that you create can be edge to edge on the canvas in Photoshop and After Effects, but any critical elements in the background that you want to make sure your viewers will see need to fall within the title safe area. There are a few options for safe grids in Photoshop.

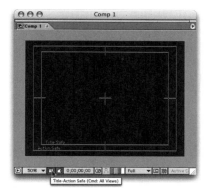

- Starting in Photoshop CS, safe grids are drawn on new images using guides when you select one of the video image presets.

- With Photoshop CS2, you'll find a basic overlay action in the Video Actions set.

- There are also third-party applications that will manage safe grids for you such as Tools for Television PRO (www. toolsfortelevision.com).

- After Effects builds in a safe grid overlay in the Composition window. Clicking the Title-Action safe button toggles it on and off of your Composition window.

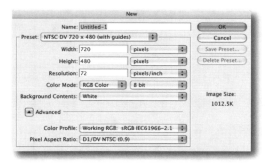

ON THE SPOT

Just My Type
Words and Symbols on the Television Screen

Most of the graphics on the air will include some kind of text, whether that be a few semi-transparent words in an effect or a block of text in a full-screen graphic for a news program or commercial.

Photoshop CS allows you to work with vector text tools to create flexible type. The advantage of vector type over raster type is that it can be infinitely scaled without losing quality. Vector type sits patiently, willing to let you edit it again and again without losing any quality or disrupting any of the other layers—even if layer styles assigned to it. Photoshop's Type tool is so powerful, many producers are using it exclusively to create titles for their programs.

Tips in this chapter will help you get the most out of the Type tool, which is a heck of a lot. We've also included some basic design concepts; after all, the Type tool only does what you tell it to do.

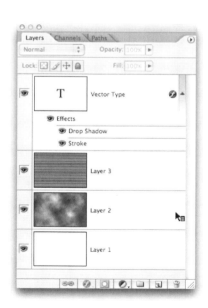

Down in Front

The foundation of typography is the font, the set of specifically styled characters. Most are text characters, while some, like Wingdings, look more like clip art images. Several fonts came with your computer's operating system. You can remove and install fonts from your computer, and whatever fonts are loaded in your system will be accessible in Photoshop. Fonts can make or break a project, so it's not uncommon for a production house to have thousands of them. However, you should have no more than 100 loaded at any time. Having too many fonts loaded can severely limit your entire system's performance, not to mention slow Photoshop down.

Photoshop runs through the list of installed fonts each time it starts, so the more fonts you have installed, the longer you stare at the feather on the startup screen.

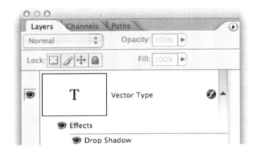

Types of Fonts: The Breakdown, Part 1

Fonts can be broken down into two distinct groups: the serifed and the sans serifed. A serif is the fine line finishing off the main stroke of a letter. Sans serif literally means "without serif," and these fonts are evenly-weighted and can appear cleaner, especially when comparing small fonts. Many people prefer serifed fonts, and for print purposes they are great, but when you use them in video you've got to be careful. The serifs are often very thin and can cause some pulsing or shimmer on TV screens. If you can sell your client on a sans serif font, you may avoid some annoying problems.

Sans serif fonts compress text into small spaces nicely, and are easy on the eyes when broadcast. A viewer may prefer to read serifed fonts in print, but for video sans serif is the way to go.

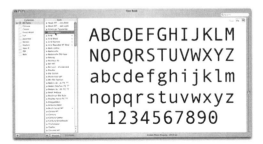

The Breakdown, Part 2

We can break fonts down a bit further—into two more groups: traditional and modern. Traditional style fonts are what you probably read every day. They are serifed fonts with a diagonal stress, and they're great for large bodies of printed text. Traditional are based on handwriting styles. Some examples are Times New Roman and Goudy.

Modern style fonts are probably useful for most video work. They sometimes have serifs, but not always. The have a vertical stress, which makes them more legible when compressed into small amounts of space. These fonts look great when used as large headings. Some examples of modern fonts are Verdana and Georgia.

What? All These T's Are Faux!

The line of 'T's under the type options is an area that many people overlook. The first two are the Faux Bold and Faux Italic buttons, which bold or italicize your text characters. If the font you're using has a bold or italic style, you should definitely use that, but for fonts that don't have those styles, this sometimes works pretty well.

Next you've got buttons for All Caps, Small Caps, Superscript, Subscript, Underline, and Strikethrough. These are not incredibly useful in broadcast video applications, but they're there if you want to try them on your text.

1. Select the Type tool.

2. Click a button in the Characters Palette.

3. Type some text.

4. To remove or change the formatting, highlight the text and click the appropriate button.

An even easier shortcut, Ctrl+clicking (contextual-clicking) on any selected text will bring up several of these options, along with Spell Check and Find and Replace commands.

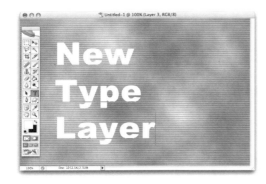

Jotting It Down

Creating and editing type in Photoshop is simple.

❶ Open a new image.

❷ Select the Type tool from the toolbox.

❸ Click somewhere on the image and type.

❹ Select the new text with the Type tool.

From here you can change the color of the text, the placement, and loads of other options. With the text selected:

- Move your mouse pointer away from the text until it becomes a Move tool. Click and drag to move the text around the document.

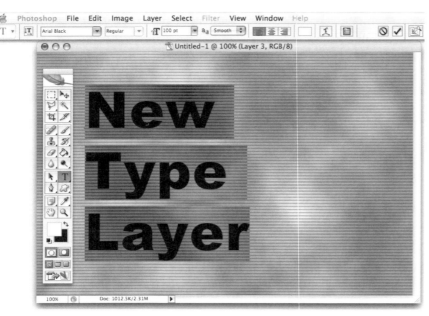

- Click the Text Color setting in the Options bar to open a color swatch and change the text's color. Since the text is highlighted, it's hard to tell if the color is what you want, so click Cmd+H (Ctrl+H) to hide the highlighting while you choose a color.

- Change the font, orientation (horizontal or vertical), size, anti-aliasing options, alignment, and style in the Options bar at the top of the screen.

- Click the Commit Current Edits button in the Options bar or press Return (Enter) when you're finished.

- Edit the text again at any time by selecting it with the Type tool.

Give It Some Character

The Character Palette offers complete control over the look of your text. To open the Character Palette select Window>Character or click the Character Palette button in the Options bar. Leave your text selected (if it's not selected, just choose the Type tool and Ctrl+click (contextual-click) in the document and choose Edit Type) and you can make any of the following adjustments.

- Font – Change the font of your text.

- Font style – For fonts with italic, bold, bold italic and other options.

- Font Size – Again, with the text selected, you can change this value and see the change immediately.

- Leading – pronounced "ledding," this value indicates how much room will be between carriage-returned lines of text. Auto usually gets you close, but you can always adjust this manually to get the look you want.

- Kerning – Use this setting to increase or decrease the amount of space between two characters. Place your cursor between the two characters in the offending space or lack thereof, and use this field to change the value. A quicker way to do this is to hold Option (Alt) and use the right and left arrow keys. Avid editors may be confused by this term, as Avid uses it for tracking.

- Tracking – This setting controls the overall space between each letter, the tightness of the line of text. You can make adjustments with this field or by highlighting the entire line of text and using the Option+arrow key (Alt+arrow key) method.

- Horizontal and vertical scaling – Not all that useful, since vector text can be transformed to perfection without losing quality, but here if you need it nonetheless.

- Baseline Shift – For exponents or scientific notations. Highlight the character you need to shift and adjust the value in this field.

- Color – Another place to change the color of the text. Remember Cmd+H (Ctrl+H) hides the selection so you can see the color.

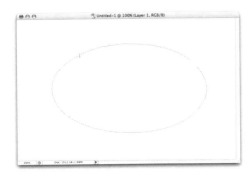

The Path to Greatness

So you want to create text that follows a custom path? Well, it's simple. You can make your type follow any vector path.

❶ Create a path using a Shape tool or the Pen tool (you can also make a selection and choose Make Work Path From Selection at the bottom of the Paths Palette).

❷ Switch to the Type tool.

❸ Place your mouse pointer over the path.

❹ The Type icon changes to a Type on Path icon.

❺ Click the path and type.

❻ Your text follows the path.

❼ Delete the shape layer.

Following the Path

Once you get the text created, it's also easy to move it around the path.

❶ Choose the Path Selection or Direct Selection tool.

❷ Move it over the type.

❸ Click and drag to move the text along the path.

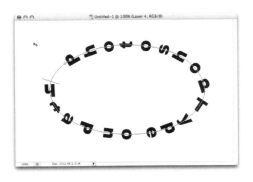

The Horizontal and Vertical Type tools create different looks when typing on paths.

● The Horizontal Type tool creates text that runs perpendicular to the path.

● The Vertical Type tool creates text that runs parallel to the path.

Scrolling Through Fonts

Want a preview as you scroll through your fonts to find the perfect one? Sure you do. You never know exactly what font is going to look best. Try this method to see what each font looks like very quickly.

❶ Select the text.

❷ Use the keyboard shortcut Cmd+H (Ctrl+H) to hide the selection.

❸ Click inside the Font Family selection window.

❹ Use the up and down arrow keys to scroll through the fonts.

❺ Hit Return (Enter) to exit the Font Family selection window when you're done.

Font Efficiency

So now you know what font you want to use, but you've got multiple layers of text to change. Save some time by changing them all at once.

❶ Select one layer of text in the Layers Palette.

❷ Turn on the link icon next to the other layers in the Layers Palette or if using Photoshop CS2, Cmd+Click (Ctrl+Click) to select multiple layers.

❸ Select the Type tool, but do not click in the document to activate any type.

❹ Holding shift, select the new font family from the menu in the Options Bar.

❺ All layers change.

This works with all the Options Bar settings.

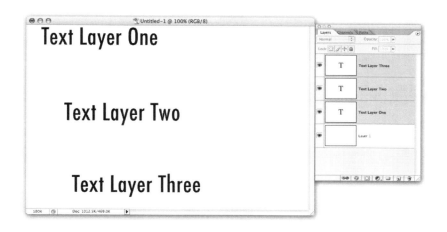

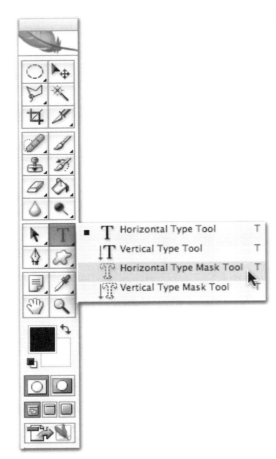

Text Shaped Selections

Holding the Type Tool icon down opens a menu containing both horizontal and vertical Type tools and horizontal and vertical Type Mask tools. Type Mask tools make an active selection based on the outlines of vector text. With a type selection you can stroke or fill just the selection to create a new bitmap layer, or use the type selection in another layer.

1 Select the Type Mask tool (Horizontal or Vertical).

2 Create a new layer. Activate the layer by clicking its name in the Layers Palette.

3 Click anywhere on the document. The document is covered with a color overlay.

4 Type your text.

5 The text shows up white, giving you a preview of your new selection.

6 Click the Move tool to deactivate the Type Mask tool.

7 Your Type is now the active selection. The selection can now be moved, copied, transformed, filled, or stroked.

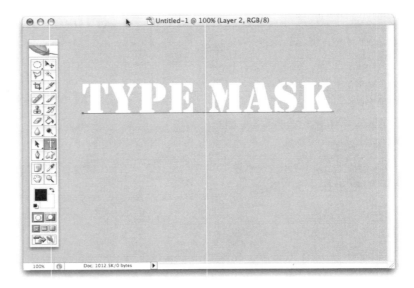

Copy This Down

As this chapter's introduction noted, many producers use Photoshop instead of their NLE's title tools. Misspelling a word is an embarrassing mistake TV producers can't afford to make. Luckily, Photoshop offers a few ways to help avoid typos.

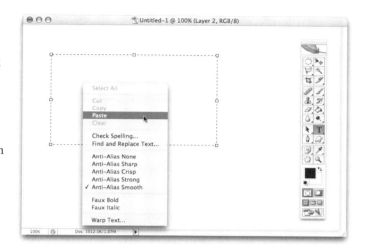

Use Photoshop's Copy and Paste Function

❶ Select and copy text from a document in your word processor, from a web page, etc.

❷ In Photoshop select the Type tool.

❸ Click and drag to create a selection box. Your type will auto-wrap to fill this box.

❹ Select Edit>Paste to paste the text into the selection box.

❺ If necessary, choose Select>All, then adjust font family and size values.

Use Photoshop's Built-in Spell Checker

❶ Ensure you have a dictionary selected in the lower portion of the Characters Palette.

❷ Select the text to be checked.

❸ Select Check Spelling. Alternately, Choose Edit>Check Spelling.

❹ Add or ignore words the spell checker doesn't recognize just like you would in a word processor.

Seek and Destroy (or at Least Replace)

You may need to change a single word or number that appears in several layers of type. For example, say you're finishing up a graphic for an event only to find out the date or location has changed. Photoshop's Find and Replace command comes in handy in situations like this.

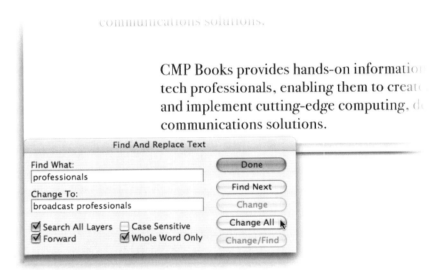

1 Make sure all layers you want affected are shown and unlocked. If you want to protect a layer from the Find and Replace changes, hide or lock it.

2 Select a non-type layer (like the background, for example).

3 Choose Edit>Find and Replace Text.

4 Type the what you want to replace in the Find What box.

5 Type what you want to replace it with in the Change To box.

6 Select Search All Layers and Whole Word Only.

7 Select Change All.

If you want to change only part of a document's text, use the Forward setting. It searches forward from an insertion point you leave active in the text. Whole Word Only will restrict Photoshop from changing text that is part of a bigger word.

Screen Safety, Part 1

Don't forget to keep your text inside the title safe areas. Photoshop CS can automatically create guides to show you where the title safe areas are. To make a new document with title safe guides:

❶ Select File>New.

❷ From the Preset menu select the proper sized document for the project you're working on (see your NLE's documentation). For example, for NTSC DV projects, choose NTSC DV 720 x 480 (with guides).

❸ Select OK. Your document opens with an action safe area (outer box) and a title safe area (inner box).

❹ Temporarily hide the guides by pressing Ctrl+H selecting View>Extras.

If using Photoshop CS2, be sure to check out the new Video Actions from the submenu of the Actions Palette.

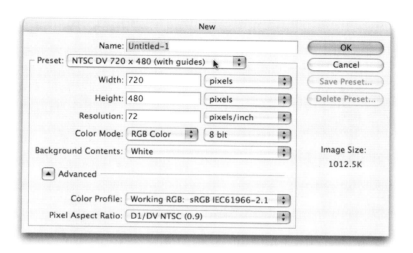

Screen Safety, Part 2

For broadcast video you've got to be careful with your color selections. When you want white, use an off-white color with a value no higher than 235 in the RGB color picker. Blacks should be no less than 16 on the same scale. Keep your colors safe for the screen to avoid muddy darks and burning lights.

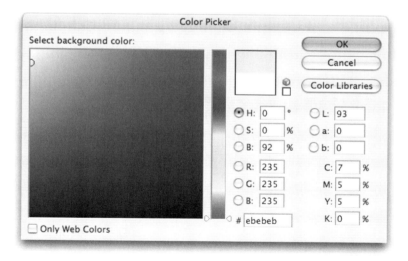

Smooth It Out

Using an anti-aliasing method on your type is almost always a good idea. Anti-aliasing blends the edges of the text to make a smoother effect. Anti-aliased text looks clean and smooth, it's less likely to create noise on TV screens, and it's easy to create.

1 Select the Type tool.

2 Select an anti-aliasing method from the Options bar or the Characters Palette

3 Change the anti-aliasing method by selecting the text and changing the setting

You'll notice the difference between the None setting and any of the others, but the other four may produce only a subtle difference in your text. Experiment to find what you like best.

Layered Text Effects

Using the Type tool and the Layers palette you can create some pretty cool text effects. Here's a simple example. Keep in mind type layers are vector based, so many filters require first rasterizing them, or turning them into pixels. Don't worry, Photoshop will do this for you – with your permission, of course.

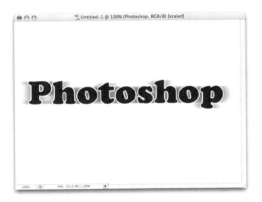

1 Create a text layer by selecting the Type tool and typing "Photoshop."

2 Duplicate the layer by pressing Cmd+J (Ctrl+J). The copy appears above the original.

3 With the original (lower copy) selected, choose Filter>Blur>Motion Blur.

4 A dialog opens asking if you want to rasterize the type. Select OK.

5 Enter a value of around 60 in the Motion Blur settings dialog and press OK.

6 In the Layers Palette, drop the blurred layer's opacity to about 70%.

7 Add a small stroke to the copy layer to complete the effect.

Styles For Miles

You can dramatically alter your typed characters with Layer Styles. These include drop shadows, strokes, color and pattern overlays, glows, and bevels. Layer Styles are powerful because they update with the type even after you transform size or perspective. To apply Layer Styles:

1 Double click the text layer you want to apply styles to.

2 A huge dialog comes up. Select which Style effects you want to add.

3 Photoshop gives you a preview in the document.

4 Click OK to finalize effects and exit the Layer Style dialog.

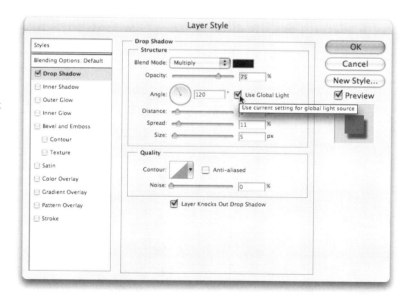

Drop That Shadow!

By default, the drop shadow you apply to each layer follows the lead of the first you set, the global light. The angle of the shadow will default to the global light angle value. When you change this in a subsequent layer, Photoshop will change the shadow's angle on all layers. This is often to your advantage, but you can circumvent it by clicking Use Global Light in the Drop Shadow submenu.

Solo Shadows

You can put an object and a copy of its drop shadow on separate layers. This is handy when you want to transform the shadow independently from the image and can produce an interesting perspective effect.

❶ Activate a layer.

❷ Click Cmd+J (Ctrl+J) to duplicate the layer.

❸ Double click the lower copy and add a drop shadow in the Layer Styles dialog.

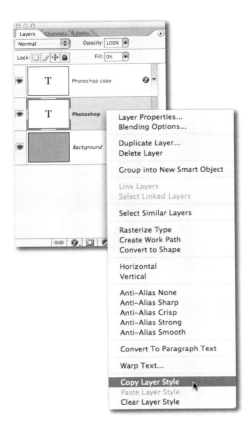

❹ Return to the Layers Palette and drop the lower layer's fill to zero. The layer disappears but the shadow remains visible.

❺ Transform the object to skew the shadow.

Do It Again!

Once you apply a style to one layer, it's easy to apply the same style to other layers in the same document.

❶ In the Layers Palette Ctrl+click (contextual-click) the layer with the Layer Style applied .

❷ Select Copy Layer Style.

❸ Ctrl+click (contextual-click) the layer to which you want to apply the style.

❹ Select Paste Layer Style—or, to apply the style to multiple layers, Ctrl+click (contextual-click) and select Paste Layer Style to Linked.

And In Closing...

We'll wrap this chapter up with some general tips about graphic design. If you're interested and have time, consider reading further into the art of graphic design. Until then, keep these basics in mind.

- Avoid setting information in all caps. It may seem like a good idea, but it makes things more difficult to read.

- You don't have to fill the entire screen with words. In fact, it's best if you don't. Leave some room for that text to breathe!

- Beginners center everything. Try some left or right justified text (left is more commonly effective). When used with the right graphic elements, this can make a big difference.

- Don't overdo it. Beginners like to use every font on the machine in one full-screen graphic. Keep it simple, but more importantly keep it consistent.

- Create repetition in your elements. Use the same image for bullet icons, elements of the same graphic for accent, etc. Make your elements look like they were designed to complement one another.

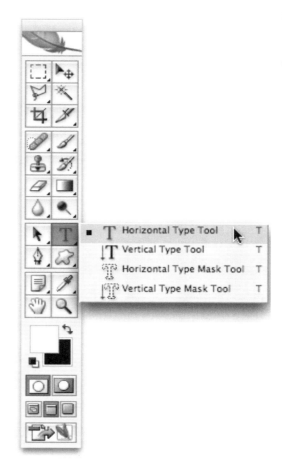

ON THE SPOT

CHAPTER 7

Type in Motion
Using the After Effects Type Engine

Text plays an important role in television graphics whether it's communicating important statistics or the score of the basketball game. Clear, readable text gets the job done. As viewers get more sophisticated, they expect their screen graphics to evolve as well. When used properly, dynamic text engages the viewer and can capture and hold their attention.

Looking to put your text into motion? Then it's time to switch over to After Effects. If you're new to AE or on a deadline, there are nearly 300 Animation Presets to get you started. When you're ready to dig in, there's a wealth of tools that can generate powerful results. Let's get started on the path to better text animation.

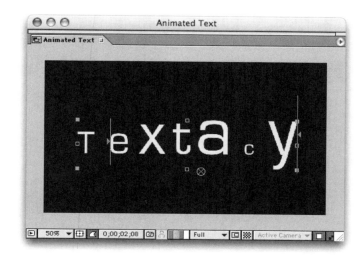

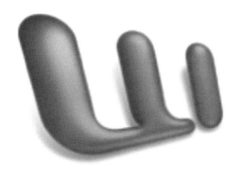

Input – Avoid Spelling Errors

The first step to animating text is getting the text in. Since you probably didn't study secretarial or data entry skills... why make things hard, just copy and paste!

1 Open up the script or storyboard, and then select the text. If using a word processor, run the spell-check first.

2 Press Cmd+C (Ctrl+C) to Copy the text.

3 Switch to After Effects and create a new Text Layer by pressing Cmd+T (Ctrl+T).

4 Click to make the text insertion point active.

5 Press Cmd+V (Ctrl+V) to paste the text in.

Morphing Letters or Shapes

Need to do a simple "morph" on an object (and no we don't mean at the level of T2). Well you can use Adobe Illustrator and After Effects, it involves using pasted paths.

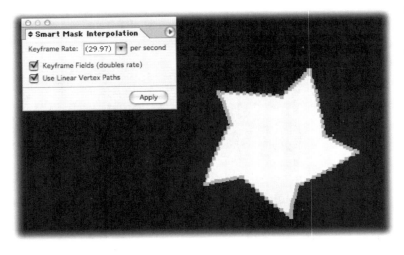

1 Paste the first shape using the method described in the tip Input – Illustrator Paths.

2 Add a keyframe for the Mask Shape property and leave it highlighted.

3 Move your playhead indicator to the point in time you want the morph to finish.

4 Press Cmd+V (Ctrl+V) to paste the shape.

5 RAM preview the comp... chances are the morph is jagged.

6 Select your two keyframes and choose Window>Smart Mask Interpolation.

7 Set your keyframe rate to match your comp settings... for best results also check the Keyframe Fields option.

8 Click Apply then RAM Preview the results.

Input – Illustrator Paths

Sometimes you'll want to bring text (or simple shapes) over from Adobe Illustrator. These can be pasted inside of After Effects and animated via keyframing the mask shape. But the process is a little tricky.

❶ In Adobe Illustrator, press Cmd+K (Ctrl+K) and check the following preferences:

Switch to the File Handling & Clipboard Preferences.

Choose to Copy as AICB (no transparency support).

Check the Preserve Paths option.

❷ Create Text or a Simple Shape.

❸ For text you need to create outlines. Select the text object then choose Type>Create Outlines or press Cmd+Shift+O (Ctrl+Shift+O).

❹ Copy the paths to your clipboard by pressing Cmd+C (Ctrl+C).

❺ Switch to After Effects.

❻ Create a New Solid by pressing Cmd+Y (Ctrl+Y). Specify color and size, and then click OK.

❼ Paste the paths into your new solid layer by pressing Cmd+V (Ctrl+V).

❽ To view the paths (which are handled as masks), select the Solid Layer and press MM to reveal the masks and their properties.

❾ Keyframe the Mask Shape to create dynamic character animation.

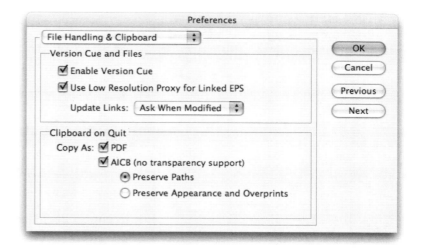

97

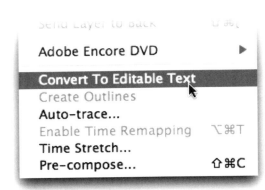

Input – Photoshop Type

We love Photoshop as much as the next designer (okay... we may love it too much). Photoshop has awesome controls for everything, especially text. Except designing text in Photoshop was not such a good idea if you intended to animate the text, as it came in as all one piece and rasterized (not a good idea if you intend to scale and move it around). But fortunately Adobe caught on and fixed this in After Effects 6.5.

1 Build your text inside Photoshop using all of the Paragraph and Character formatting controls you need. However, stay away from layer styles, as you'll be better off adding those in AE for animated text layers.

2 Import your PSD file as a composition.

3 Select the text layer(s) and choose Layer>Convert to Editable Text.

4 Begin to animate.

Input – Illustrator Layers – Part I

How many times have you typeset a bunch of text in Adobe Illustrator, only to have it import as one big blob? (It's okay... it's happened to us). The key is to split your text into (non-nested) layers.

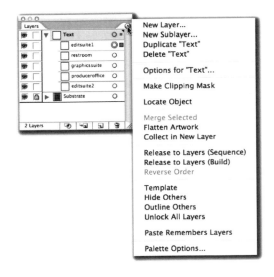

To import each line as a layer:

1 Open your Layers Palette in Illustrator.

2 Locate the layer that contains your text.

3 Twirl it down to see the nested layers.

4 From the Layers Palette submenu (the triangle on the side) choose Release to Layers Sequence (to put one on each layer) or Release to Layers Build.

5 Drag the layers out of the set so they are independent (and not indented).

6 Rename layers so they are easier to identify, and then save your document.

7 Switch to After Effects.

8 Import as a Composition.

Input – Illustrator Layers – Part II

If you want to do very complex animations, it can help to have each letter split out to its own layer. To import each letter as a layer, you'll need to do a little extra prep work:

1 Select all Text elements and convert them to Outlines by choosing Type>Create Outlines or pressing Cmd+Shift+O (Ctrl+Shift+O).

2 Open your Layers palette in Illustrator.

3 Locate the layer that contains all of your text.

4 Twirl it down to see the nested layers.

5 From the Layers palette submenu (the triangle on the side) choose Release to Layers Sequence (to put one on each layer) or Release to Layers Build (to perform an additive build).

6 Drag the layers out of the set so they are independent (they'll no longer be indented).

7 Rename layers so they are easier to identify, and then Save your document.

8 Switch to After Effects.

9 Import as a Composition.

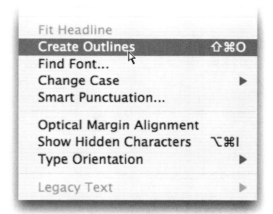

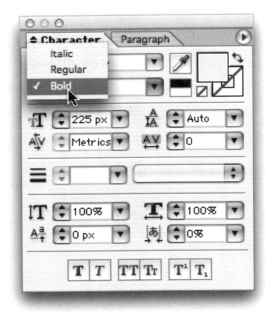

Flicker Fix

Interlaced displays (and rendering) are great for smoothing out fast-moving objects... but they are brutal on thin text. If you plan to animate text, you'll need to make sure to avoid thin serifs or lines that shimmer on screen. Here are a few options to try.

- Go Bold – If the font has a Bold, Heavy, or Black version, try it. Chances are that will solve your problem.

- Faux Bold – While it's less desirable (typographically speaking), the Faux Bold option will thicken your font a bit. You enable it at the bottom of the Character Palette.

- Feathered Edges – You can also add a soft-feathered edge to your text. Experiment with a drop shadow effect set to the same color as your text. Set the Distance to 0 (zero) and adjust the Softness setting to taste.

- Sans Serif – Some fonts are better suited for the screen than others. Try using a Sans Serif font (without the curvy hooks), which may be better suited to your needs.

- Motion Blur – Try enabling Motion Blur. Remember to turn it on globally for the comp (the M icon at the top of your timeline) and locally for the text layer (the M checkbox).

- Directional Blur – Try adding an adjustment layer (Layer>New>Adjustment Layer) and applying a Direction Blur Effect (Effect>Blur & Sharpen>Directional Blur). Leave the angle at 0 (zero) and set the Blur Length to a low value. RAM Preview and adjust.

IMPORTANT: You can only judge interlace flicker when previewing a Full-Size Comp at Full Quality that you have sent out to an interlaced television display. Be sure to use After Effect's Video Preview ability to view your comp on a video display.

Loosen Up

If you plan to animate text character-by-character, the text needs a little breathing room. Be sure to set the tracking to a higher value for best results.

❶ Select the text layer.

❷ Call up the Character Palette.

❸ Adjust the tracking numbers between 10 – 50 for best results.

Discover Text Animation Via Presets

Looking to wrap your head around After Effects powerful text animation tools? Then be sure to check out the animation presets that began shipping with After Effects 6.5. You'll find nearly 300 built-in animation presets that show off what AE can do. Be sure to check out the sample movies by choosing Help>Text Preset Gallery. When you find one you want... it's simple to put the animation into action.

❶ The text layer must be a live After Effects editable text layer. Highlight the desired layer.

❷ Call up the Effects & Presets window.

❸ Twirl down the Animation Presets Folder.

❹ Pick a category and an animation.

❺ Double-click to apply the preset to a highlighted layer, or drag-and-drop.

❻ The animation will begin near your current time indicator.

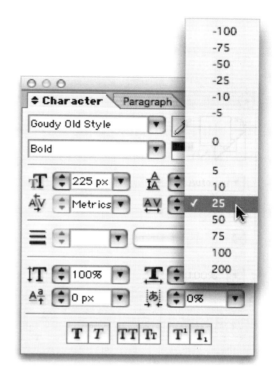

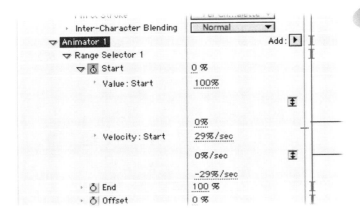

Getting More Animations

Just because After Effects comes with presets doesn't mean the effects are "canned." There are several ways to modify them.

- Combine text presets to create new combos.

- Twirl down and access the Animator controls. Pay particular attention to the Selector controls.

- Twirl down the advanced tab and change the Randomize Order command to On. You should also try changing the Shape of the Animator (there are six choices).

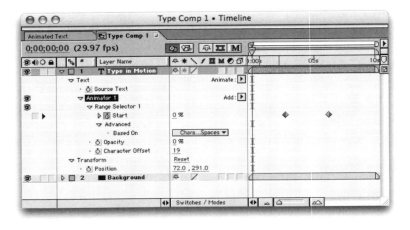

Looking For a Better Time

Not happy with the timing of the animation presets you've chosen? Don't worry about it... it's a quick fix!

1. Select the text layer you need to modify.

2. Press U to see all of the User added keyframes.

3. Most animations will have two or four keyframes. Set the first keyframes where you want the animation to start and the last keyframes where the animation should end.

Note: You may also want to take advantage of keyframe interpolation to create smooth transitions between animation states.

What's the Point (or Paragraph)?

Depending on your needs, you're going to have to choose between Point Text (independent lines of text) or Paragraph Text (text within a bounding box that you can choose alignment and justification for).

- Point Text: Just click and type.

- Paragraph Text: Click and drag a bounding box first. Then you can click within and type.

But what if you change your mind? Don't worry... it's not a problem!

❶ With the selection tool, select the text layer. (Note, you can't convert a text layer that is in editing mode).

❷ With the text tool selected, context-click inside the Comp window.

❸ Choose Convert To Paragraph Text or Convert To Point Text. NOTE: Make sure all characters are visible in a paragraph box before converting. When converting from paragraph text to point text, a hard return is added at the end of each line

❹ For Paragraph Text, click within the new text layer and resize the handles of the bounding box.

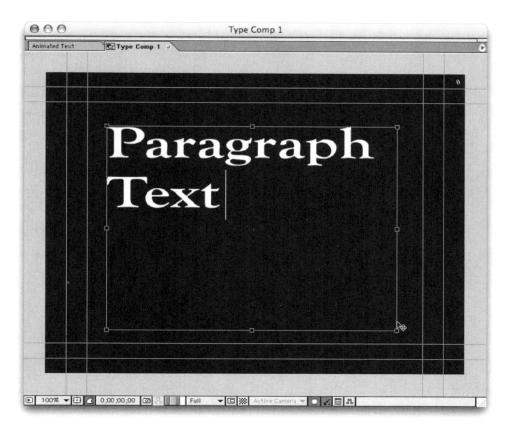

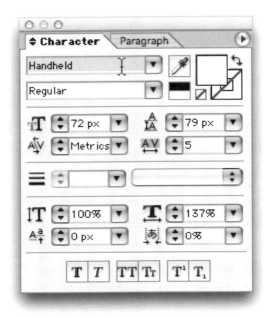

Decisions...Decisions

Trying to pick the right font? Here are some quick tips to make trying new fonts easier.

- Have a highlighted line of text? Then it's hard to see color and changes due to the inverse effect caused by the selection. Choose View>Hide Layer Controls or press Cmd+Shift+H (Ctrl+Shift+H) to disable this reversal.

- What's my name again? Call up the Character palette and click in the font name field. You can use the Up and Down arrows to select fonts.

- If you know what font you want, just type its name in the Name field of the Character palette.

Feet and Inches

Want to be a typography snob (or at least fit in with the Art Director)? Take a look at that key next to the enter or return button. That's the feet and inches mark. If you need true quotes or apostrophes, it takes a little more work. Adobe calls these 'smart quotes' and you need to know where to find them.

❶ Call Up your Character palette.

❷ Choose Use Smart Quotes from the Character palette sub-menu (the triangle icon).

❸ Use the Feet and Inches key, After Effects will substitute Quote marks, Single Quotes, and Apostrophes as needed.

Gain Your Composure

Want better looking paragraph text, but don't have a lot of time? Then let Adobe do all the work. By using the built-in composers, After Effects can analyze lines of text and make adjustments in spacing to optimize a pleasant arrangement on the page. This will result in less weird spaces and avoid hyphenation.

- Single-line Composer: This standard approach composes text one line at a time. This is best if you want manual control over how lines break. This method will try to compress, rather than expand text to make the best fit.

- Every-line Composer: After Effects identifies possible breakpoints, and then evaluates them to produce the best results.

To choose a Composer, select it from the Paragraph palette submenu.

D.I.Y. Animations

So you've tried the presets, maybe even tweaked a few... and now you feel ready to make your own text animations. While there are a lot of controls to be concerned about... a little bit of knowledge combined with a sense of adventure can get you through.

1. Select the text you want to animate in the Timeline window or choose specific letters in the Comp window.

2. Choose Animation>Animate Text and select a property from the submenu. You can also use the Animate pop-up menu, located in the Timeline window.

3. In the Timeline window, adjust the property values to taste. We suggest changing one at a time and previewing your results when you are first starting out. Don't forget about using keyframes.

4. Contract or expand the Range selector. Use keyframes for Start or End of the Range Selector. You can also animate the Offset property to move the Selector 'through' your animation.

5. Further refine the selection and animation by using the Advanced options.

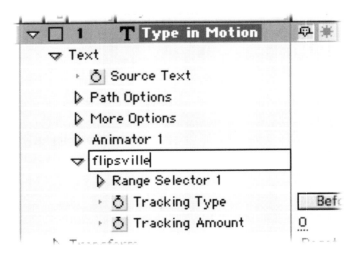

Keep Your Place

When you add an animator group, it gets the incredibly descriptive name of Animator. While factually correct, it doesn't go a long way in the style or func[ ] department.

❶ Select the Animator in your Timeline window.

❷ Press Return (Enter) to make the name active.

❸ Type a new name in that is more descriptive of the animator.

❹ Press Return (Enter) to apply the name.

Save Your Place

Looking to keep your new animators for future usage? It's an easy process. First create your animation as previously described.

❶ Select your animator in the Timeline window.

❷ Choose Animation>Save Animation Preset.

❸ Store the animation preset in an easy-to-find location, generally this will be in your After Effects preset folder.

Lose Your Place

If you've animated a text layer, and it just didn't work out, then you better get a fresh start. As easy as it was to add an animator, you can clear them out as well.

➊ Select the text layer in the Timeline window.

➋ Choose Animation>Remove All Text Animators.

If you want to get rid of a single animator, then select it in the Timeline window and press delete.

Always Kern

We've never met a font that we didn't want to kern. Getting the spacing right in your text is an important (and often overlooked) step. The goal is to achieve an optical balance to the text, such that if you were to 'pour water' over the text, it would flow evenly between the characters. Always take the time to kern; it will raise the professionalism of your graphics.

➊ Click between two characters that you want to kern.

➋ Hold down the Option (Alt) key.

➌ Press the left arrow key to tighten the kerning or the right arrow to loosen the kern.

➍ Release the option key and continue to move through the text with your arrow keys. Repeat the option (alt) + arrow key combination as needed.

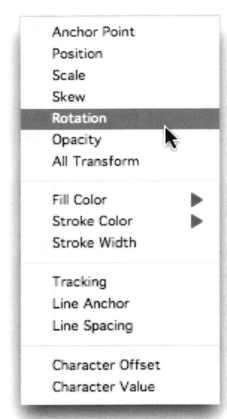

What Can Be Animated?

Animators can be used to achieve a lot of different results. Understanding the list of options is the first step to getting results. Many of the animators achieve results identical to other layer properties, however there are plenty that are unique.

- Position – The position of the characters can be moved in combination with the range selector.

- Skew – How much the letters slant. The Skew Axis specifies the axis along which the character skews.

- Fill Color – You can use RGB, Hue, Saturation, Brightness, and Opacity to modify the colors of the text.

- Stroke Color – Similar to the Fill Color modifications.

- Stroke Width.

- Tracking – The space between all characters in the text.

- Line Anchor – This is to specify the alignment when tracking. A value of 0% is a left alignment, 100% is right alignment, and 50% will track from the center.

- Line Spacing – The space between lines.

- Character Offset – This will roll the characters forward to the following or proceeding letter or number. This is useful for decoding text or performing odometer type effects.

- Character Value – Allows for the replacement of letters with the selected character.

- Character Range - When using Character Offset or Character Value property, you can limit it with a range. You can opt to Preserve Case & Digits to keep characters in their respective groups.

When Good Presets Go Bad

Have you ever picked a text preset just to have nothing happen? You double-check the sample movie... but nothing you do seems to make the Animation Preset work. It pisses the heck out of us too, but we've finally found some answers. What's going on?

The text animation presets were created in an NTSC DV 720x480 comp. There were also built using the Myriad Pro font set to a point size of 72. Differences in comp and point size may mean you have to make changes. Not a big deal... things are easy to fix.

Try these techniques individually or in combination until you get the expected results.

Solution 1: Enable Motion Blur

Many of the presets use blurring to create their motion effects.

❶ Ensure Motion Blur is turned on for the Composition by clicking the M at the top of your Timeline.

❷ Check the Motion Blur switch next to the type layer.

Solution 2: Make the Text colors match

Check the sample movies and look at the text animation sample movie. You should set the stroke and fill to match what you see in the movie. Many of the animation presets rely on the stroke setting to work, and if you don't have a stroke at all... many presets won't work at all.

Solution 3: Adjust the text animator's position values

If the text disappears unexpectedly, you need to adjust the text animator's position values in the Timeline or Composition window. Twirl down the text layer for more precise control.

Solution 4: Retype it

If the characters change dramatically, just type your text in again. You'll also want to check your settings in the Character and Paragraph palettes.

Lights and Optical text animation presets (6.5)

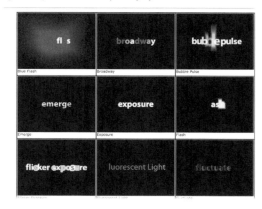

109

Random Is Good

Animator groups include a default Range selector. This specifies which characters or section of a text layer will be affected. One of the easiest ways to modify an animation is to randomize it. This will ensure different, but cohesive results when reusing an animation preset throughout your show.

1 Select your text layer.

2 Click on the Add Menu and choose Add>Selector>Range.

3 Twirl down the Range Selector then Advanced.

4 Change the several different properties to see results... pay attention to the following in particular:

- Randomize Order – This will randomize the order in which the property is applied to the characters specified by the Range selector.

- Random Seed – This affects the method used to calculate the random order. If reusing an animation, change the Random Seed number to get a different result.

- Shape – This will affect the shape used to select characters between Start and End of the range. The shape affects how the selector moves between. Choosing different options will result in gentle, but significant changes. You can specify Square, Ramp Up, Ramp Down, Triangle, Round, and Smooth.

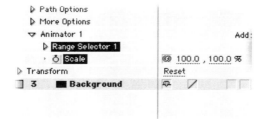

Wiggle It

You also can use Wiggly selectors to create selections that "wiggle." This will generate variety in what animates and how it animates.

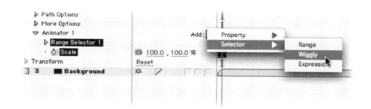

- Mode – How selectors combine together with the other selectors above it. This is most similar to how multiple masks combine to achieve complex results.

- Max and Min Amount – How much variation is allowed.

- Wiggles/Second – The amount of wiggles or cycles per second.

- Correlation – How much the variations are correlated to each other. With a setting of 0%, characters wiggle independently, with 100% they wiggle in unison.

- Temporal and Spatial Phase – You can choose to modify wiggles by time (temporal) or per character (spatial).

- Lock Dimensions – Choose to scale dimensions equally in all directions or independently. This is most useful for properties such as scale.

Need More Fonts?

Looking for some affordable (or even free) fonts? Here are a few of our favorite websites to get more fonts. Check them out for several free and affordable new type faces that are well suited for broadcast graphics.

- www.chank.com

- www.fonthead.com

- www.chankarmy.com

- www.fontalicous.com

- www.girlswhowearglasses.com

- www.acidfonts.com

- www.myfonts.com

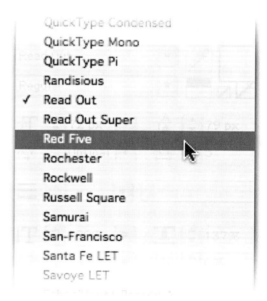

ON THE SPOT

Keep It Legal
Making your Images Broadcast Safe for the Screen

If you've worked in a broadcast station, you know what happens to those who let their graphics slip outside the broadcast safe range (if you don't work in TV, let's just say it involves burly engineers and old, rusty pieces of video gear). But seriously, it's important to keep your graphics within spec.

There are many different techniques when working with After Effects and Photoshop, and you'll need to learn most of them. Different situations require different approaches, so let's take a look at some real-world solutions to keep your graphics safe.

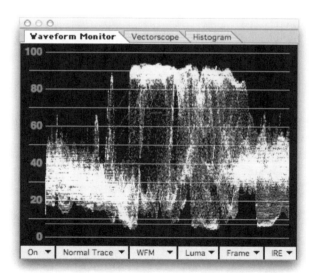

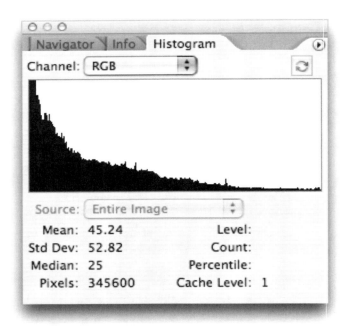

That Layer Is Well Adjusted

Whether you are working in Photoshop or After Effects, an adjustment layer is the way to go. These non-destructive layers allow you to apply an adjustment such as an image command (in Photoshop) or an effect (in After Effects) to multiple layers at once. These adjustments are non-destructive and only affect those layers below the adjustment layer. If you need speed and flexibility (who doesn't?) then choose an adjustment layer.

Histogram

Need scopes inside of Photoshop? Well there aren't any built-in, but one palette can do the trick.

1 Choose Window>Histogram.

2 From the submenu, specify Expanded View.

3 From channel choose Luminosity.

4 You can now monitor your graphic. It is important to keep the black levels (left edge) above 16. The white levels should be clamped below an RGB value of 235.

Interlace Flicker Fix

When televisions were invented, the original intention was to get the frame rate to match up with the rate that electricity was cycling in our walls... but that didn't really work out. To compromise, it was decided that there would be the same number of interlaced fields... which produced smoother motion on video displays. However, interlacing has introduced some new problems. Whenever the video or graphic signal contains very thin lines (generally less than 2 pixels), a visible flicker is annoyingly present. Never fear though, both Photoshop CS2 and After Effects offer solutions.

In Photoshop CS2:

1. Open up the Actions Palette (Window>Actions).

2. From the Actions Palette submenu choose Video Actions.

3. Select Interlace Flicker Removal.

4. Press Play.

5. Be sure to analyze the new image on a video monitor. Continue to adjust as needed.

In After Effects

1. Go to the topmost layer of your composition.

2. Press the Home key to assure you are at the beginning of your comp.

3. Choose Layer>New Adjustment Layer.

4. Choose Effect>Video>Reduce Interlace Flicker.

5. Adjust Softness Slider as needed.

6. Preview the results at Full Quality.

7. Be sure to analyze the new image on a video monitor. Continue to adjust as needed.

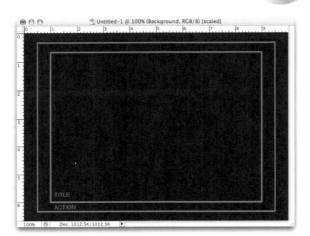

Action Safe – Get in the Picture

You're going to need to keep your video elements in their place (and we don't mean yell at them until they behave). It's important to keep both title and action safe in mind when designing. Otherwise your elements will get cut off when they hit the video screen. There are several methods to mark this area off, here are the two easiest:

Use a Template

The built-in video sized presets all have the action and title safe areas marked out. These are added as guides to the new document. If they disappear, choose View>Show>Guides or press Cmd+; (Ctrl+l).

Use an Action

Looking for a more permanent set of guidelines? Photoshop CS2 comes with an Action called Title Safe Overlay. Just open the Video Actions from the Actions palette. Running this action will add a guide layer to the top of your document. Just remember to disable its view before saving.

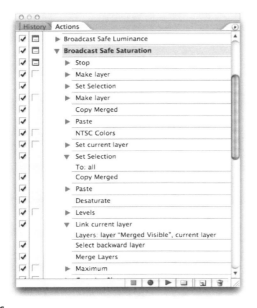

A Better NTSC Safe

Sure, Photoshop has a built in broadcast safe filter (Filter>Video>NTSC Colors) but we've never been very happy with it. This filter produces clipping in the affected areas as it has no rolloff command and can produce visible edges where it "fixes" your image. So what's a thoughtful designer to do? Work around it of course! In Photoshop CS2, Richard Harrington wrote an action to fix broadcast safe colors.

1 Choose Window>Actions.

2 Load the Video Actions from the Actions palette submenu.

3 Select Broadcast Safe Saturation.

4 Press Play.

Need a Vectorscope?

If you've hung out with an engineer long enough (or actually paid attention in class) you know the importance of a vectorscope to check your graphics. While hardware scopes are great, they can set you back a pretty penny. If you are looking for a software vectorscope to check your graphics, you don't need to go very far.

VideoScope – www.evological.com

This Mac-only product is an affordable option at only $30 US. This software waveform and vectorscope uses your computer's video input ability. It can perform real-time luminance and chrominance analysis. You can also drag a QuickTime compatible still (such as PICT, TIFF, TARGA or PSD) into the RGB video window to analyze it.

EchoFire – www.synthetic-ap.com

This tool has long been regarded as an essential. While Photoshop CS2's ability to send video out over FireWire slightly diminishes EchoFire's value, it does not eliminate it in any means. If you can afford the $255, it's a great tool for those with video devices or output cards. Besides being able to view your active AE or PSD file, it can also overlay waveform monitor, vectorscope, and test patterns on the video preview. EchoFire also comes with a Video color picker that lets you preview your color choice on the video monitor. It will also "legalize" the chosen colors for broadcast use.

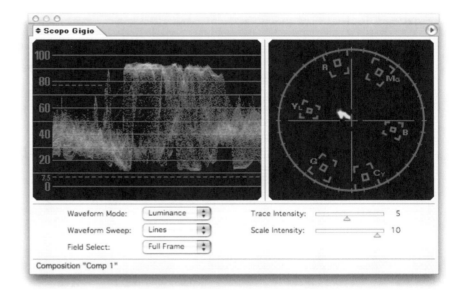

Scopo Gigio – http://www.metadma.com

A simple but useful scope that we just found. Cross platform and works in both Photoshop and After Effects. Available for $50 for Photoshop and $75 for After Effects. Definitely worth trying out.

I Can't Read the Text

When designing video graphics, there is a minimum font size you should follow. This is dictated by both readability factors and legal issues. Certain graphics such as election or car commercial info has a minimum height of a certain number of scan lines. But text is measured in points right? Well, it doesn't have to be.

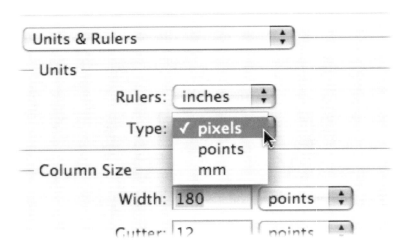

In Photoshop

❶ Open up your preferences by pressing Cmd+K (Ctrl+K).

❷ Choose the Units & Rulers category.

❸ Switch Type to pixels.

❹ Design away. The scanline rule is equivalent to pixel height when designing with non-square pixels in Photoshop CS or newer.

In After Effects

❶ The default measurement is already pixels for type.

❷ Design as needed, scanlines is equivalent to pixels for a non-square pixel composition.

Color Cast...Fast

Ever have a picture (or several pictures) where the lighting is just "off?" You get a distinct color cast to all of the images that you need to remove. Don't worry, Levels has got you covered there as well.

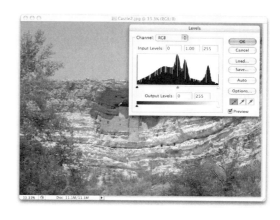

❶ Examine your photo to identify a suitable white and black point.

❷ Add a Levels adjustment layer.

❸ With the black eyedropper, click on the darkest point in the picture. It's okay if there is color spill in the shadows.

❹ With the white eyedropper, click on the lightest point that should be white.

❺ Adjust the middle slider (gamma) to taste.

❻ Click OK.

Better Exposure

After applying a Levels adjustment, it's easy to fix poor exposure. The essential step is to view your image data with a histogram. This is done in Photoshop within the Levels Dialog box. In After Effects, be sure to open the Levels command in the Effects Editor, not the Timeline.

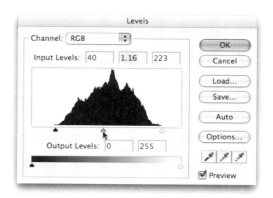

❶ Pull the white input slider into the left, until it is at the point where the histogram start to rise. This will restore brightness to the white areas.

❷ Pull the black input slider into the right, until it is also at the point where the histogram rises. This will restore contrast into your blacks. While a separate command exists for brightness and contrast, the levels adjustment lets you perform several improvements with one adjustment, thus cutting down on quantization (loss of quality) introduced from multiple image processing steps.

❸ Now it's time to modify gamma. The middle slider can be used to change the intensity of the midtones, without making dramatic changes to the highlights and shadows. This leads to a better exposure of the image.

❹ When satisfied, click OK.

Broadcast Colors in AE

If you need to make your colors broadcast safe, After Effects is the way to go. The Broadcast Colors effect alters pixel color values so the layer or comp is ready for the television screen. You do not want to send a signal amplitude above 120 IRE units to a consumer set. By using an adjustment layer, we can quickly fix our AE composition.

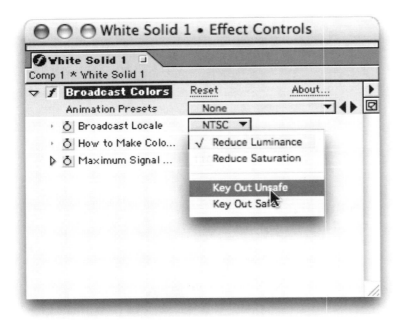

❶ Choose Layer>New Adjustment Layer.

❷ Place this layer at the top of your layer stack and ensure that its first frame begins at the start of your comp.

❸ Choose Effect>Video>Broadcast Colors.

❹ You now must choose whether to make the signal safe by either reducing saturation or luminance. Reducing saturation takes a greater amplitude modification than reducing luminance, and will therefore alter the appearance of the graphic more.

❺ Use the Key Out Unsafe and Key Out Safe if you'd like to see which areas are affected. This however is not an end solution, just a viewing option. Make the background color a contrasting choice (lime green anyone?) so you can see where the problem spots exist.

❻ Set the Broadcast Local to match your broadcast standard. You can choose between NTSC (National Television Systems Committee) the North American and Japanese standard or PAL (Phase Alternating Line) which is used in most of Western Europe and South America.

❼ Specify the Maximum Signal in IRE units that you can allow. The range is 100–120 IRE. A level of 100 is generally overkill and produces noticeable shifting. A level of 120 however can be considered risky as you are riding the maximum edge. So as Goldilocks would say, "110 IRE units is just right."

Color Master Control

Being able to detect problem colors is an important skill. It's also not easy to do without a scope or other hardware device. However, a few best practices on your part can help limit the number of close calls you find yourself in.

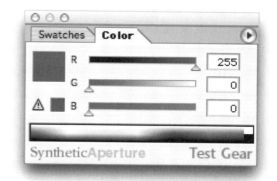

- A non-broadcast-safe image means that part of your picture has exceeded the safe level limits. This will result in an undesirable color shift on televisions.

- You should avoid using pure black and white values. The most commonly accepted levels for black and white are 16 and 235 respectively.

- You should avoid highly-saturated colors such as pure red or yellow. A value of R=255 mixed with G=0 and B=0 will produce a visible smear on a television. Try to avoid overly-saturated colors.

- You should always render a test movie at the highest quality your system can playback in real-time. Be sure to send this signal out to a professional video monitor or a consumer television (better yet, both). This will help you show the color shifting errors that occur with certain colors and luminance ranges.

Compressed Files = Trouble

As a wise man once said, "Don't cross the streams." Very bad things happen when you do...It is a bad idea to mix still image compression with video compression. Always keep your still images in an uncompressed format like a PSD or uncompressed TIFF. The use of JPEGs (or worse yet, GIFs) can cause all sorts of weird problems. Just stick with high quality images as sources and you'll get a cleaner signal all the way through.

Color Swatch Palette

Need consistent colors when designing across multiple workstations? Then use a big box of "crayons." By creating a custom color palette and saving swatches, you can ensure that all designers are using your station's or show's colors.

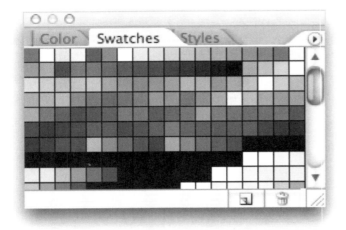

- Choose Window>Swatches to show the Swatches palette.

- By default, Photoshop has an assortment of swatches loaded (122 to be exact).

- Option+Click (Alt+Click) on a swatch to delete it.

- Load a new color as your foreground color. You can select colors from an existing document with the eyedropper tool.

- Click in an empty area of the Swatches palette to add a swatch.

- Name the swatch when you add it to provide further clarification to the designer.

- From the Swatches palette submenu, you can save the swatches. The default location is the Photoshop application folder>Presets>Color Swatches. These files can then be copied to the same location on another computer.

Mixing Video Sources with Still Graphics

If you need to mix video stills or freeze frames into your Photoshop designs, then you need to do a little extra prep. Otherwise video artifacts may get in the way of your finished designs.

1 When opening an exported freeze frame from a video application, be sure Photoshop CS is correctly handling the pixel aspect ratio. Choose Image>Pixel Aspect Ratio and select the correct number for your acquisition format.

2 You should de-interlace your freeze frame if the original source was interlaced footage. Choose Filter>Video>De-Interlace.

3 Choose to eliminate Odd or Even fields (depending upon which part of the motion you want to keep).

4 Fill the missing fields in with the Interpolation method.

5 If placing the frame into video graphics that you are designing with full RGB levels, you'll need to restore the black and white points. Apply a Levels adjustment and bring the Input levels into 16 for Black and 235 for white.

Highlight Tamer – Select Color Range

Have a hot spot you need to fix? You can use color range to get that fire out.

1 Choose Select>Color Range.

2 Choose Highlights.

3 Click OK.

4 Choose Select>Modify>Feather... soften 4-10 pixels.

5 Choose Layer>New Adjustment Layer>Levels. Adjust the Gamma and White Point as needed.

Tweaking Skin Tones

Need to tweak color cast or skin tones? You can always click the auto button in the Levels dialog box, but if that doesn't work, it's time to make tweaks at the channel level.

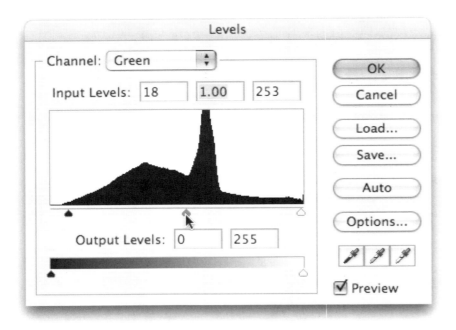

1 Add a Levels adjustment layer.

2 Switch to the Red channel by pressing Cmd+1 (Ctrl+1). Move the black and white sliders in towards the center (to right where the histogram starts to rise). Adjust the gamma slider as needed. It will be difficult to see proper color until all three channels are adjusted.

3 Switch to the green channel by pressing Cmd+2 (Ctrl+2). Repeat the histogram adjustment.

4 Switch to the blue channel by pressing Cmd+3 (Ctrl+3). Repeat the histogram adjustment.

5 Switch back to the composite view by pressing Cmd+~ (Ctrl+~). Tweak the three input sliders to fix contrast and exposure.

6 You may need to switch back to an individual channel to further tweak. Usually the adjustment will be to the gamma.

7 When satisfied, click OK.

Shadow/Highlights Quick Fix

Have a really dark image? Well the best option is to re-shoot or re-scan. But what if that's not an option? Well you could try the new Shadow/Highlight command to attempt image rescue. The purpose of the adjustment is to help salvage images where the subject is silhouetted due to strong backlight. It can also be used to improve subjects who have been washed out by the key light.

① Open an image that is too dark.

② Choose Image>Adjustment>Shadow/Highlight... (there is no adjustment layer for this command). Since this is a destructive editing command, you should work with a duplicate file or layer so you can return to the original photo if needed.

③ Click the Show More Options box to expand the power of the tool. Be sure the Preview box is checked.

④ Adjust the Shadows and Highlights.

- Amount – How intense of an adjustment is made.

- Tonal Width – Small values affect a smaller region; larger values will begin to include the midtones. If pushed too far, you'll have halos around your image.

- Radius – A tolerance setting that looks at neighboring pixels to determine the affected area.

⑤ Apply Image Adjustments to improve image quality.

- Color Correction – Modifies the saturation of the adjusted areas. This allows you to counterbalance washed-out images.

- Brightness – If working with a grayscale image, Color Correction is replaced by a control for Brightness.

- Midtone Contrast – This command affects missing contrast in the midtones of an image. Negative values reduce contrast, positive values increase contrast.

- Black Clip and White Clip – Raises the black point of shadows and lowers the white point of highlights.

⑥ Click OK.

Photo Filters

If you've ever shot pictures or video with color filters in front of the lens, then you'll appreciate the Photo Filter adjustment layers that were added to Photoshop CS. While these are not nearly as good as the flexible nik Color efex, they can achieve several important looks.

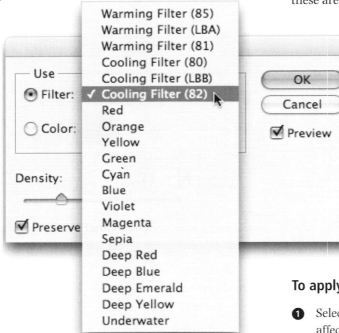

- Warming Filter (85) and Cooling Filter (80): These are meant to even out photos that were not properly white-balanced. The Cooling Filter (80) makes images bluer to simulate cooler ambient light. The Warming Filter (85) makes images warmer to simulate hotter ambient light.

- Warming Filter (81) and Cooling Filter (82): These are similar to the previous filters but cast a more distinct color. The Warming Filter (81) makes the image more yellow and the Cooling Filter (82) makes the image bluer.

- Individual Colors: The Photo Filter also has several preset colors to choose from. These can be used for two primary purposes: 1) To add a complementary color to a scene to remove color cast, or 2) To introduce a color cast for stylistic reasons.

To apply a Photo Filter:

❶ Select the top-most layer that you want to affect. (All layers below will be affected).

❷ Choose Layer>New Adjustment Layer>Photo Filter. Be sure the Preview box is checked.

❸ Select the Color Option by choosing a preset or defining a custom color.

❹ If you don't want the image to darken from the adjustment, be sure to check the Preserve Luminosity box.

❺ Adjust the Density slider of the effect.

❻ Click OK.

❼ To modify the effect, just double-click on the adjustment layer's icon.

Straighten Images

The world is not flat, and sometimes it shows. Thin, crooked lines look very bad in video. If a photo is not straight (because it was shot or scanned at a slight angle), it is easy to fix.

❶ Access the Measure Tool (I) and find a surface you think should be horizontal (or vertical).

❷ Click and drag a line to measure the angle.

❸ Select Image>Rotate Canvas>Arbitrary. The correct value is inserted automatically from the Measure Tool.

❹ Crop the image or patch the gaps and make any additional repairs.

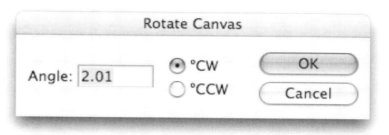

Fixing Flicker During Scan

If you are scanning in previously printed items such as newspapers, magazines, books, inkjet prints, etc, you will likely get a moiré pattern. This is caused by Photoshop scanning the small spaces between the previously printed dots. Most scanners have a de-screen filter in their software. If available use it when scanning previously printed items.

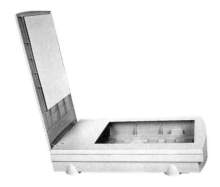

Test Gear in AE

If you are serious about getting great color and sticking to technical specs while working in AE, then you need to check out Test Gear from Synthetic Aperture. Sure, many of these tools can be found in an NLE or through hardware, but it's great to be able to work right within After Effects and feel confident with your compliance to broadcast standards. Test Gear comes with nine key additions to AE.

- Waveform Monitor and Vectorscope

- Histograms – You can view a histogram palette for red, green, blue, and luma.

- Color Picker - This adds a color picker using RGB, HLS, HSB, web-color, and grayscale pickers. Non-broadcast safe colors can be flagged and legalized with a single click.

- Color Swatch Books – You can load Photoshop color swatches ensuring consistent colors between multiple systems.

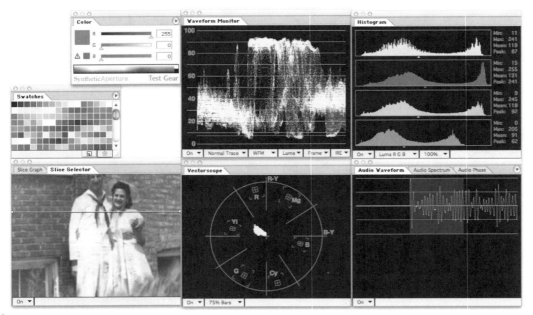

- Image Slice Display – This is a more accurate way to analyze part of an image than using an eyedropper.

- Audio Waveform Display – This give you an overall view of your audio tracks. It also allows for flagging levels that are close to clipping.

- Audio Phase Display

- Audio Spectrum Analyzer – This can be helpful to find audio cue points.

Import to Avid Systems

When importing graphics into Avid editing systems, you need to be aware of which color space the graphics were created in. Avid will ask you if the graphic has RGB (0-255) or 601 (16-235) levels. The answer may seem obvious, but it's not.

Photoshop

If you are designing in Adobe Photoshop, by default you'll have RGB levels. Therefore import with RGB levels.

However many designers choose to add an adjustment layer to their graphics to make them broadcast safe. If you've clamped your levels to fall within the range of 16-235, then you should import your graphics with 601 levels.

After Effects

By default, After Effects works in RGB space. The best solution for Avid users is to render with an Avid codec. The Avid codec will take over and ensure that the Avid correctly interprets both color and alpha data. To download the latest versions of the Avid codecs visit the Avid web page. The codecs keep moving depending on updates. We find it safest to visit http://www.avid.com/onlineSupport/ where you can click the Downloads and Updates button. From the next page just search for codecs, the latest version should be first on the results list.

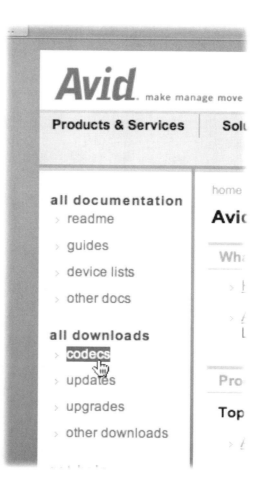

ON THE SPOT

CHAPTER 9

Pulling the Key
Solutions for Chroma Key on a Deadline and a Budget

The chroma key wall has come to be used for much more than just the weather. With improvements in both keying technology and cameras, it is possible to get professional results on tighter budgets. However, better tools don't mean much if you don't know how to use them!

This chapter offers tips on both the acquisition of footage as well as using Keylight and other plug-ins to achieve great keys inside of After Effects. Whether it's for a broadcast spot or the latest promo, proper use of chroma key technology can significantly add to your graphics and design capabilities.

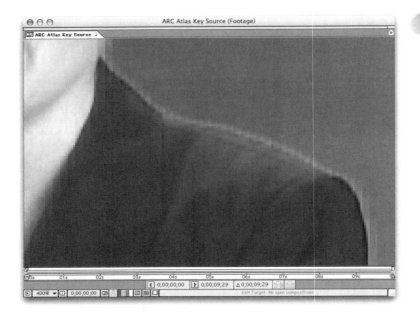

Green with DV

Everyone has his or her own beliefs when it comes to keying. Here's one more... If shooting DV, then definitely go green. The DV compression noise is present more in the blue channel, making your edges harder to get clean, than with a blue-screen. In DV, the green channel also has nearly twice as much information as the blue channel, as it is carried in the luminance stream.

By Jayse Hansen, http://www.xeler8r.com

When Your Camera is Fighting You

Often cameras, especially prosumer rigs, will have auto features turned on that can make keying much more difficult. Be sure to turn off Auto exposure, auto-white balance and auto-focus. If any of these are left on, this means the green you're trying to key will constantly be changing as your model moves. Even if you've hired a professional videographer, don't make assumptions. Double check that he or she has turned these things off or you will spend hours trying to fix it.

While you're in the setup menu, be sure to turn off Sharpening. Most consumer cameras have a sharpening filter that is turned on by default. This causes your edges to increase in contrast and destroys subtle edge detail. Turn this off.

By Jayse Hansen, http://www.xeler8r.com.

Chroma Smoothing DV Footage

By its nature, the DV format is heavily compressed. This compression introduces color artifacts, which can ruin the color in that carefully lit green screen. It can also cause major problems around the edges of your talent.

Solution #1:

Don't shoot DV. Go for beta or even DVCPRO50 if at all possible to avoid DV artifacting.

Solution #2:

If you must use DV, you'll need to do some chroma smoothing.

① Add an adjustment layer above your blue/greenscreen footage.

② Add a slight Gaussian Blur to the adjustment layer (two to four pixels).

③ Change the adjustment layer's blending mode to Color.

④ Pre-compose the footage and adjustment layers.

⑤ Proceed with your key.

Background Check

When keying, it can be difficult to judge the quality of a key when it's composited over a backdrop. Detail in the background might hide flaws in the key. You can view the key more accurately by temporarily replacing the background layer with a garishly colored solid. Make the solid color the opposite color from the original screen color. For example, if the original image was shot against a green screen, try laying it over a red solid. Be sure to check the key by moving the current time indicator to check the key at a few points in time.

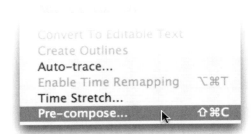

The More Mattes the Merrier

Sometimes one keying effect isn't enough. For instance, you might need one effect to deal with solid foreground objects and another effect for edge details. If this is the case, use your keying effects to generate grayscale mattes, not color images with missing backgrounds.

1 Use multiple copies of the footage and generate the mattes (this can often be accomplished within the effect by changing what you view).

2 Then combine all the mattes into a single matte, via a pre-compose.

3 Combine separate mattes using layer-blending modes. Try the screen and multiply modes, which will combine blacks and whites respectively.

4 Use the pre-comp as a track matte for the original color image.

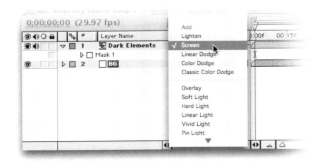

Luminance "Keying"

If you're trying to knock out a black or white background, there may be a better solution than keying: layer blend modes. If the background is black, try using the Screen mode. This will allow anything lighter from an underlying layer to show through the black. If the background is white, try the multiply mode, which will allow anything darker on an underlying layer to show through the white.

Magenta Reduces "Separation Anxiety"

If you're going to be keying on green, consider adding a Magenta "rim" light. This is especially useful if you don't have a lot of distance between your model and your screen. Add a rim light behind her. It can either be hidden directly behind her on a light stand or chair, or placed above and behind her. A default white light will suffice, but even better is one with a magenta gel over it. Why? Because the magenta is the exact opposite of the green you're trying to key. Separation is greatly enhanced.

By Jayse Hansen, http://www.xeler8r.com

Getting the Best Key

When using any keyer, you really need to switch your layers to Best Quality. It's also not a bad idea to view the comp window at Full resolution. Keying involves the finest detail of pixel manipulation. While it will slow you down a bit, you'll get much better results and color samples when working with higher quality view settings.

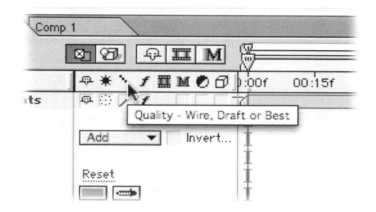

Go Shallow when Shooting

When you're going to shoot chroma key, be sure to do so with shallow depth of field. There are a number of ways to do this. If you can change your aperture settings, an aperture of 2.0f is much better than 22f. This has to do with depth of field.

You want the background as blurry as you can get it so that wrinkles, seams and hot spots blend away. Also keep your model and your camera as far away from the screen as possible. Even if it means non-green edges are showing in the shot. You can crop these out later.

You can also ensure shallow depth of field by moving your camera away from your model and zooming in on him or her. Just make sure you only use your optical zoom and not your digital zoom. (The latter will be interpolated and result in horrible edge detail.)

By Jayse Hansen, http://www.xeler8r.com

More Shooting Tips

- Turn down exposure to reveal hotspots: We've heard lots of odd ways to reveal your hotspots when setting up your screen lighting. We've found the best way is to simply set the exposure of your camera down and look through the monitor. Your hotspots will be glaring at you.

- Light with two softboxes, or two fluorescent lights: These are lights for the screen only. These lights are separate from the lights you use for your model. You can fix a lot with even lighting by two identical soft boxes or even two or three long fluorescent light fixtures. Soft boxes are incredible, yet expensive. Shop-light fluorescent lighting fixtures are incredibly cheap; available at any hardware store. burn cool, and work great. Their only drawback is that they can sometimes cause a subtle hum in your audio.

- Avoid fast movement: Quality keyers have gotten a lot better about handling motion blur. But if you can avoid it. Do so. This is typically where the "give-away" happens. This is where a good key can fall apart, especially in DV footage.

- Go Progressive: Fields definitely get in the way of a good key. If your camera shoots progressive, take advantage of it.

Keylight: What the...?

What is Keylight? Keylight is The Foundry's powerful chroma keying plug-in that comes free with the Production Bundle versions of After Effects 6. It won the Academy Award for Technical Excellence, and it's a one-stop-shop for keying, despill and color correction.

When you apply Keylight to a layer and choose a color to key out, two things happen: Keylight erases all the pixels that match the key color and it also removes traces of that color (spill) from the other pixels. So if you key out green, all green (or near-green) pixels will turn invisible, and the rest of the pixels will have their greenness reduced.

By Marcus Geduld

Keylight: Where the...?

Okay, you've installed AE 6.0 or 6.5, imported a green screen shot, added it to the timeline and chosen Effect>Keying from the menu, only to find that you don't have the Keylight plug-in installed. Unfortunately, this gem of a keyer doesn't install automatically with After Effects. Not to worry, though. Just pop the AE6 installation CD back into your CD-drive and find Keylight in its own folder with its own installer. Also included in this folder is a Keylight manual in Adobe Acrobat format. While you are there, be sure to install the Digital Anarchy 3D Assistants as well.

By Marcus Geduld

Keylight: Pick Your Color Wisely

The first thing you should do after applying Keylight is to choose the Screen Color (the color that will be removed and despilled). To do so, click the eyedropper by Screen Color, and then click a background color in the image.

Note that you can't add to the Screen Color by repeatedly clicking in different parts of the image, so just click once on a pixel that is representative of the general color in the background. If too much background is still visible (or too much is gone), adjust the Screen Strength parameter.

By Marcus Geduld

Keylight: Seeing in Black and White

If you switch the View to Status, all pixels will display as black, white or gray. Black pixels are completely transparent. White pixels are completely opaque. Gray pixels are see-through (partially transparent/partially opaque). This view allows you to easily see problems in the matte. In general, it's good to have some gray pixels around the edge of the foreground (so that hairs and other semi-transparent elements can blend into the background), but the background should be solid black and the foreground should be solid white.

By Marcus Geduld

Keylight: You Don't Need a PhD

With nearly 60 parameters, you could easily confuse Keylight with the cockpit of a 747. Not to worry, there are only a few main controls you'll need to adjust. The rest are for fine-tuning.

After selecting the color to key out (Screen Color), adjust Screen Strength until all of the background is gone and foreground is completely visible.

To see the matte Keylight is creating, choose Screen Matte from the View parameter dropdown (when you're finished looking at the Matte, remember to set the View parameter back to Final Result).

If there's too much spill (too much of the background color in the foreground), increase Despill Bias until you've fixed the problem. You may notice that as you remove more spill, the foreground image starts to become transparent. This is because Despill Bias, which controls spill removal, and Alpha Bias, which controls the transparency of the foreground, are locked together by default. If you uncheck Lock Biases Together, you can despill without knocking out the foreground.

By Marcus Geduld

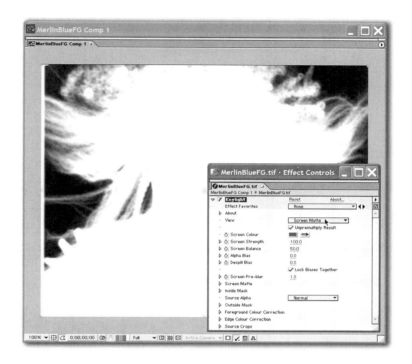

139

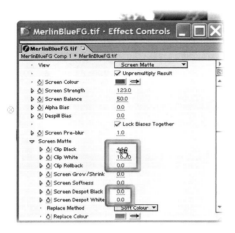

Keylight: Holey Matte!

If you twirl open the triangle by Screen Matte, you'll find a slew of controls that will help you fix matte problems. While making adjustments, you may want to toggle back and forth between Screen Matte view and Final Result view.

Clip Black makes the blacks blacker; Clip White makes the whites whiter. Sometimes when you adjust these controls, you'll find that you'll ruin the edges of your foreground. If you do, use Clip Rollback (a sort of rewind function) to undo a little of the clipping and bring the edges back.

Screen Despot White removes tiny white specks that are inside the generally black background; Screen Despot Black removes tiny black specks that are inside the generally white foreground.

Your end goal, as you view the Screen Matte, should be to have an all black background and an all white foreground, with a little bit of gray around its edges. Wispy elements, like smoke, should be gray.

By Marcus Geduld

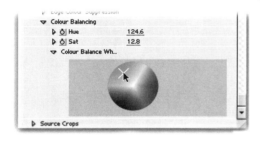

Keylight: Ring Around The Color

In addition to adjusting Saturation, Contrast and Brightness, you can also adjust Hues for both the Edge and the Foreground. You can either adjust hues numerically, by scrubbing the Hue slider (under Color Balancing), or you can twirl open Color Balance Wheel and click anywhere on the wheel to pick a new color. The foreground (or edge) will become tinted with the color you pick.

If you adjust the slider (rather than the color wheel), nothing will happen at first, because the Sat value is set to zero by default, meaning totally desaturated (no color). You'll have to raise the Sat value before you can add a hue tint.

By Marcus Geduld

Keylight: Color Me Corrected

After you've knocked out the background, you'll usually need to adjust the foreground's colors so that they match the colors of the new background plate. Keylight has two groups of color-adjustment parameters: Foreground Color Correction and Edge Color Correction.

- "Foreground" means the majority of the person or object left behind after Keylight has removed the background.

- "Edge" refers a thin band of pixels running around the person or object. These edge pixels often require special treatment because (a) they will usually contain the majority of spill from the knocked out background, and (b) they are the pixels that will be touching the composited pixels in the new background, so they're very important when you're trying to create a believable blend between foreground and background images.

- To adjust how thick a band Keylight thinks of as the edge, adjust the Edge Grow parameter while displaying the Color Correction Edges view.

By Marcus Geduld

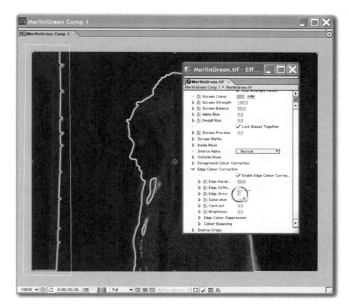

Keylight: Getting a Little Edgy

The Edge Hardness and Edge Softness parameters are not opposites. Edge Hardness controls how much the edge color correction merges into main foreground color correction, whereas Edge Softness blurs the edges.

By Marcus Geduld

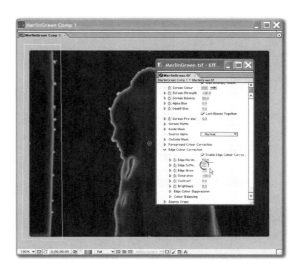

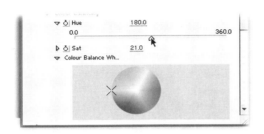

Keylight: 90 Degrees of Separation

Most AE plug-ins view color as existing on a color wheel, with red at the top and green at the bottom. You can specify colors on this wheel in degrees: zero degrees = red, 180 degrees = green, and 360 degrees equals red, because on any circle, zero and 360 degrees are in the same spot.

The Hue sliders in Keylight work the same way. Since the default slider value is zero, the default hue is red. If you scrub the slider to 180, the hue will be green. (Remember to increase Sat if you want to see Hue having any effect).

If you use the color wheel, note that it's been rotated 90 degrees clockwise. So red is facing East (at 90 degrees, whereas normally it would be North, at 0 degrees).

By Marcus Geduld

Click Close... Mask Far

When keying... remember, you don't usually need to key the entire screen out. Instead, you only need to get the areas closest to your subjects. Always click as close to the hair as you can when trying to set your key color. Likewise, if your edges are falling off, you can always use a garbage matte or mask to get the further edges.

Don't Scrub So Hard!

When you adjust properties in keying plug-ins, you need an easy hand. Slight over-adjustments can destroy edge detail or tint the image an unrealistic color. But if you hold down the Command (Control key) while you scrub any property value, you'll be able to adjust that property in tiny, subtle increments. This trick works for any property value (in the Timeline or in Effect Controls), not just those on keying effects.

Keylight: Who Was That Masked Man?

To fix holes in the foreground and opaque patches in the background, you can either use the Clip Black and Clip White parameters, or you can use mask—the type of masks you draw with the pen tools. You should only use masks if your foreground is pretty static, or you'll have to animate the mask shape.

If you use masks, make sure you change their blend modes to None in the Timeline, because you don't want the masks to actually act as normal masks; you just want them to be used by the Keylight plug-in.

To fix holes in the foreground, draw a mask just within the boundaries of the foreground object. Then, assuming this is Mask 1, select Mask 1 for Keylight's Inside Mask parameter.

You can eliminate opaque areas in the background (rigs or boom mics) by drawing a mask around them and selecting this mask in Keylight's Outside Mask parameter.

By Marcus Geduld

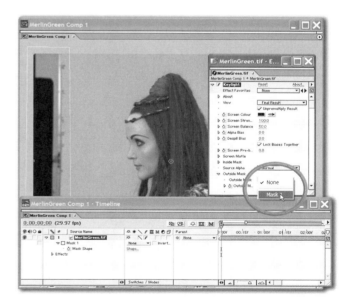

ON THE SPOT

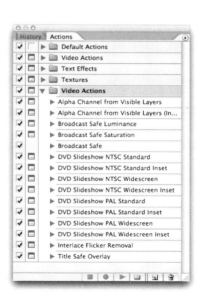

Making Deadlines
Using Automation and Scripts to Speed up Your Workflow

If you work on broadcasting, you are used to deadlines. Deadlines for air, deadlines for satellite, deadlines for deadlines for that matter. Being creative takes time, but the whole reason behind computers was so we could drive those flying cars, have robots serve us, and work those 15 hour work weeks (we're still waiting, too). So although those dreams of a utopian future have not come to pass, it is possible to do more in less time.

In Photoshop, you have several powerful tools that can boost your automation abilities, from scripts to actions, Photoshop is well-suited for cranking through a large pile of "to-do's" and converting them to "dones." Even After Effects offers some powerful timesavers to get the job done. This chapter will speed you up significantly, and we invite you to radically change the way you work.

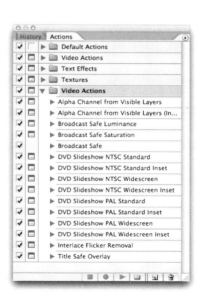

Creating Actions

Photoshop has a macro tool called Actions (Window>Actions). This tool allows you to record steps that you frequently go through when working in Photoshop. This powerful feature will save you hours and hours of time if you get into the habit of using it. Simply put, it can record any series of steps from creating new documents, applying a series of filters, resizing images, to saving files and converting image formats. Here is a quick step-by-step guide to creating an action.

1 Create a new action set by clicking Create new set at the bottom of the Action palette. (All actions must be contained within a set.)

2 Create a new action by clicking Create new action at the bottom of the Action palette. When the new action is created, you can specify which set it will be assigned to as well as a color for the action and also assign it to an F key.

3 You are now in record mode. Nearly everything your do in Photoshop now will be recorded to the action.

4 When you have run through the steps that you want to record, simply click the Stop button at the bottom of the Action palette.

You now have an action that will quickly run through and repeat those steps on other images.

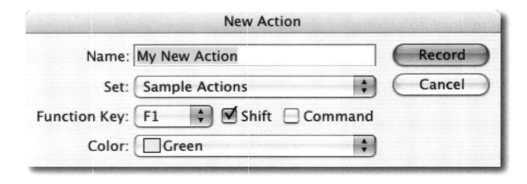

Geeks Love Buttons

Once you have built a set of custom actions, you can view them as buttons. These buttons will be colored based on the color assigned to each action. Under the Action palette menu, select Button Mode. This makes for a much more visually friendly way to view and access your actions. There are few drawbacks to viewing your actions as buttons.

- All actions in all action sets are displayed as buttons with no visual separators from one set to another.

- There is no way to edit the actions in button mode. Although, this is also a benefit in that you don't run the risk of messing up the steps in an action.

Once in button mode, if you need to make a change to an action or action set, you use the same steps to get out of button mode.

Just Do It!

Certain functions in Photoshop such as saving files, creating new images, and resizing images have dialogs that pop up when you do them. Actions give you the ability to run the action with or with out dialogs appearing. Turning on dialogs is handy if you know that you always want to feather a selection at a certain point in the action, but you want to change the value each time. However, in many instances you want to apply the same settings to the same functions each time. In this case, you just want the action to run with the settings that were applied when the action was created. You can enable and disable the dialogs by clicking the toggle dialog on/off button to the left of each action. You can toggle this on or off globally for an entire action or turn it on or off for each individual step that has a potential dialog associated with it.

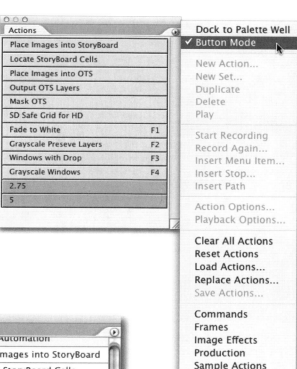

147

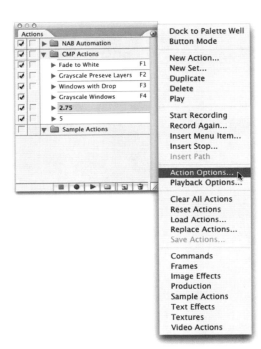

Oops, I Forgot My F Key!

Don't worry, no need to call a locksmith. All of the settings for an action, including the F key that it is assigned to, can be accessed by double clicking on the action in the Action palette. You can go back at any time and change the action's color or the F key assignment. However, you cannot change the set that it lives in from this option once the action has been created. To move an action to another set, you need to drag it from one set to another in the Action palette.

My Action Isn't Recording Everything

As you start to get deeper into actions, you may notice that certain menu items don't record as a step in an action. If the function doesn't alter the image itself, it will not be recorded to the action. To add these functions to an action, select Insert Menu Item from the Action palette menu. This will display a prompt that will ask you to choose a menu item. Once you select that menu item and click OK, that function will be recorded as a step in your action. Examples would be:

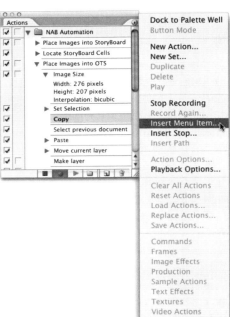

- Showing or hiding rulers

- Showing or hiding palettes

- Zooming in or out on the image

Set Up Your Preferences with Actions

One great power tip is that if you like your preference set up differently for the different types of work you do in Photoshop, you can record your preferences set one way as an action, and another set of preferences in another action. This allows you to quickly change from one preference setup to another without ever opening up your preferences dialog. Simply create a new action, open the preferences dialog and set up your preferences. When you commit to the preferences setting, those settings are saved in the action.

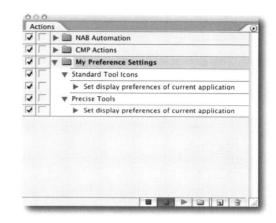

Editing and Saving Actions

Once your actions are created, you may need to make changes to them. Here are a few ways you can edit your actions.

- Change the order of the steps by dragging one step in front of or behind another step.

- Delete a step by dragging it to the Action palette trash can.

- Modify the settings of a step that has a dialog associated with it by double-clicking on that step. Change the values, click OK and the new settings are saved for that step.

- To record more steps in an action, click on the step that you want to start recording after, click the record button, and keep on going. All the things you do are recorded into the action at that location until you click stop.

- You can save your actions, only as part of an action set. Simply select the set that you want to save and choose Save Actions from the Action palette menu. You can also load actions that you have saved from this menu.

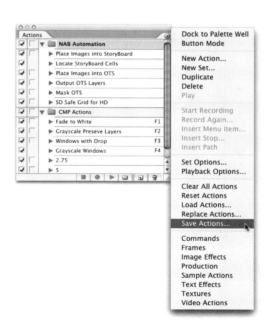

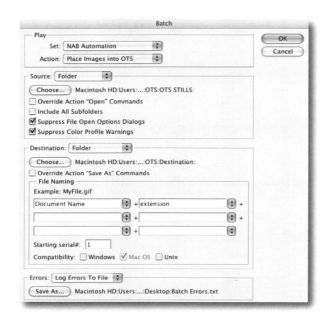

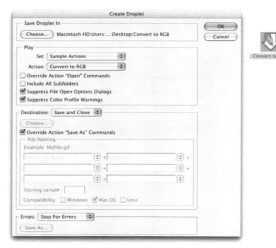

That's Cool, But I Need to Fix 1,000 Images!

So you have the killer action that you created that works magic on your images, but you have more images to run it on than you want to think about opening in Photoshop. No problem.

- Select File>Automate>Batch.
- Choose the action set that contains your action.
- Choose your action.
- Pick the source folder you want the action to run on.
- Choose the destination where you want the images saved to.
- Set the other parameters that apply to your particular use.

Photoshop will now run through the folder and batch apply the action to all of the images within your source folder and save them to your destination folder.

Is Photoshop Leaking? I Have a Droplet

Actually, this is a rhetorical question, because software can't leak. But droplets are an extension of Photoshop that are worth mentioning. Droplets are small applications that are created from an action. The steps of an action are embedded into the droplet. Once the droplet is created, an icon is created for it, and when files or folders are dropped on the icon, it will launch the files or contained files in Photoshop and perform the actions on them.

One benefit of droplets, is that once the droplet is created, the action that it was created from does not need to be installed in Photoshop for the action to run. This is handy if you have people in your art department that you want to process images with an action, but you don't want to risk having them mess up your action. Just pass them a droplet. Droplets are created by choosing File>Automate>Create Droplet.

You're Approved!

If you enjoy the power of the web as much as we do, then why not get client approval for your designs via a web page? Under the File>Automate menu you will find the Web Photo Gallery option. This option will generate a full-blown image approval web site.

❶ Choose your image source folder.

❷ Choose your destination folder.

❸ Pick your template.

Photoshop now creates a full web site that can be uploaded to your web server. Your client can see all of the images that you need approval on, and they can even make comments and have them mailed to you via the feedback options. When you are on a deadline and you just need to get images in your clients hands fast, there is no faster way to get crucial feedback.

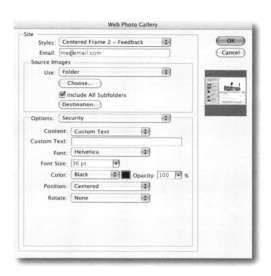

Making After Effects Render Settings

When working in After Effects, one of the most time-consuming repetitive tasks is setting up your Render settings each time you want to render a movie. To make this process less painful, you can create templates of your render settings for different types of render that you do. If you frequently render test movies at a lower resolution or with effects turned off and also render full resolution movies for your NLE with specific field orders, you can create a Render Settings Template for each of these settings. Under Edit>Templates>Render Setttings, you will find a dialog that allows you to create multiple render settings, and assign a default setting that will come up each time you initiate a render.

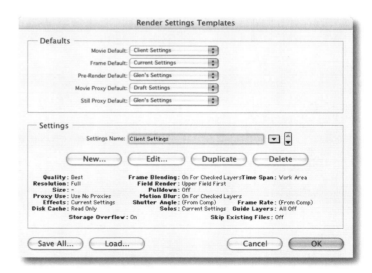

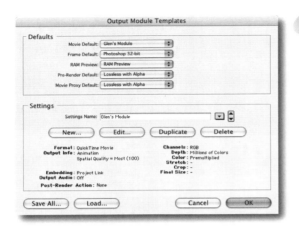

Managing After Effects Output Modules

If you are a design house working for a variety of clients, chances are they are all not editing on the same NLE. Each NLE uses a different codec, requires different audio settings, and there may be times that you need an alpha channel and times that you don't. If this is you, then creating Output Module Templates is a must. You can create an output module setting for each of your clients, their systems, and variations that will render audio, include an alpha channel, or other file output variations. This feature is found under Edit>Templates>Output Module. You can also specify the default module that will be assigned when a render is initiated.

Rendering Takes Long Enough, So Just Do It Once!

Rendering is the most time-consuming task in any compositing application. Once a frame is rendered, saving in a certain format is fast and easy. After Effects is intuitive in

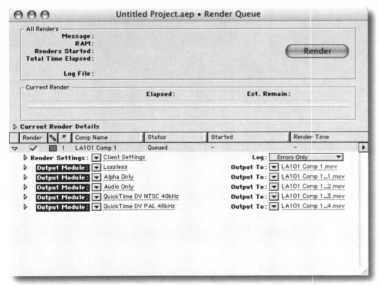

this way, by allowing you to apply multiple output modules to each render setting that you have in your render queue. Once you have added a comp to the Render Queue and specified your render settings, you can add as many output modules as you need. One for your web site, one for your NLE, and one for a CD-ROM. With the Render Queue window open and an output module selected, choose Composition>Add Output Module. This allows you to render once, and output to as many different files as you want at one time. The main consideration here is that the field order is determined by the render settings, so if you want to render a file for your Avid and Final Cut Pro at the same time, you will need to render twice because you not only have different codecs (which can be handled by multiple output modules), but the field order is different for each system. This is controlled by the render settings and you can only apply one render setting to each render.

That Depends...

One of the main drawbacks from the actions in Photoshop is that they are not conditional. This means that they do the same thing no matter what. There are some circumstances where you may want to perform one task when you have a horizontal image, and a different task when you have a vertical image.

If you are working with one image at a time, you could simply create 2 different actions and apply the correct one. But when you need to batch a large number of files at once, this solution will not work.

This is where scripting in Photoshop comes in. Photoshop is a very scriptable application, and allows you to write conditional scripts that get information from Photoshop about your images, and let you do different tasks based on what you get back. Scripting can be a very complicated process, so we won't go into details here, but you do need to know that it exists. You can script Photoshop via:

- AppleScript
- JavaScript
- VisualBasic

There are sample scripts and documentation available in the Scripting Guide folder in Photoshop's application folder.

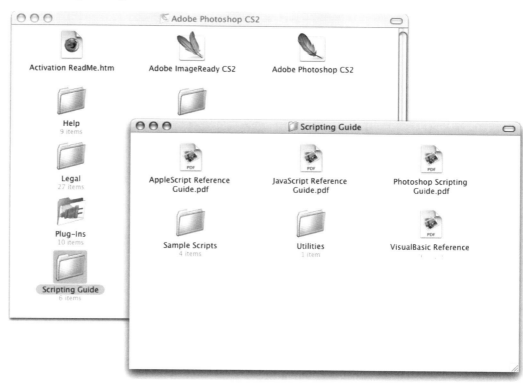

Script Events Manager

New to Photoshop CS is the Script Events Manager. This new feature allows you to run an action or a script automatically when other tasks are performed in Photoshop such as printing, saving, or creating a new document. There are a handful of pre-installed scripts that can assist you in a video environment. Since all of your artwork as video designers needs to be in an RGB color mode, you can use the Script Events Manager to convert any image that is not RGB to RGB when it is opened in Photoshop.

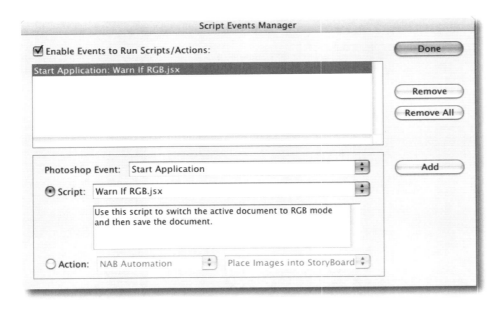

❶ Open Script Events Manager (File>Scripts>Script Events Manager).

❷ Choose Open Document for your Photoshop event.

❸ Select the "Warn If RGB.jsx" script.

❹ Click the Add button to add the event to the manager.

Now, every time you open a new document that is not RGB, a dialog will be displayed asking you if you want the image converted to RGB and saved. With a simple edit to the script (Photoshop Application Folder>Presets>Scripts> Event Scripts Only) you can disable the save routine and just have the image converted. You can add multiple events and create your own actions and scripts to be performed. This is not only a time saver, but allows Photoshop to watch out for you and catch oversights that you may miss.

Changes Are Inevitable

When deadlines either make or break you, you want to make sure that you can make changes to your documents as quickly and simply as possible. Here are a few quick tips to help you make necessary changes to documents with as little pain as possible.

- Never rasterize your layers. Text layers, shape layer, and any other vector elements should remain as vector elements, and not ratsterized.

- If you must rasterize a layer to apply a filter to it, create a copy of it first so you can get back your original text if you need it.

- Organize your layers with layer groups, color coding, and smart objects so you can easily find things that need changing. Your layer organization usually makes sense the day you create the image, but 3 weeks later it looks like a mess. The more organized it is, the faster you will be able to find what you are looking for.

- Always use layer styles and adjustment layers to modify your layers. These are editable and easily changed.

- If you find yourself using the same layer styles over and over, save them as presets in the Layer Styles palette.

- Create favorites of the effects that you regularly use in After Effects so that you can quickly recall them.

- When your client asks you to make changes, duplicate the file they want changed and name it myfile_v2. They may decide that they liked the original better, and want to keep each revision as its own file so you can quickly get back.

Third Party Automation

There are a number of resources available to you that provide tools that will speed up your design process. Here are just a few.

- Tools for Television – They offer a number of actions, add-ons, and techniques that will save you hours of time when working in Photoshop for a video project. (http://www.toolsfortelevision.com)

- Adobe Studio – A web site full of actions, plug-ins, tutorials, and tons of other resources to make you work better and faster in Photoshop. (http://studio.adobe.com)

- Just try google.com. There are literally hundreds of people sharing actions, scripts and other Photoshop related tools. Search the web and you may find that someone has already done the dirty work for you. Don't try to reinvent the wheel, if someone has done it, take advantage of the time savings and use the resources that are available to you.

I Want My Actions in the Action Menu!

You will notice that when you select the menu in the Actions palette, at the bottom of the menu there is a list of preinstalled actions sets provided by Adobe. If you don't use them and would like your action sets to appear in the menu for quick access, follow these 3 simple steps.

1. Quit Photoshop if you have it running.

2. Place your actions in the Presets>Photoshop Actions folder inside the Photoshop application folder.

3. Restart Photoshop and your actions will be listed at the bottom of the menu. Now you can quick load the appropriate sets without having to find them on your hard drive.

Even Faster Than Favorites

Did you know that in After Effects you not only can save favorite settings for your effects, but you can also copy and paste effects from one clip to another.

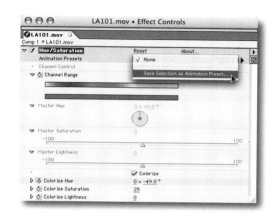

- You can copy them by selecting effects either from the Effect Controls window, or by selecting and copying them right from the timeline.

- Once you have it copied, select a different layer in your comp and paste it.

- You can also select more than one effect at a time and copy and paste it.

Quick and simple, but what a time saver!

Just Plain Work Smart

The best way to meet your deadlines is to work smart. If you find that the keyboard shortcuts in Photoshop are not logical to the way you work, or you find that there are keyboard shortcuts for things that you never use, and none for the things that you do all the time, then you need to customize your own set of shortcuts.

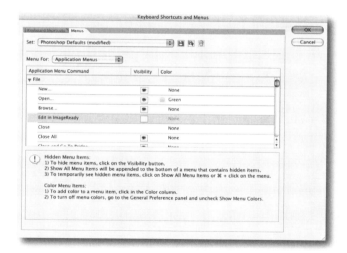

❶ Open the shortcuts editor under Edit>Keyboard Shortcuts.

❷ Here you have access to all of the functions and menus in Photoshop.

❸ Find the functions that you want to assign or change the keyboard shortcut of, and select it.

❹ Once the item is selected, simple press the series of keys that you want to assign the function to. If there is a conflict Photoshop will alert you and help you fix it.

With your keyboard shortcuts arranged in a way that makes sense to your workflow, you will find that the less you go to the mouse, the faster you will work.

ON THE SPOT

CHAPTER 11

Building Templates
Saving Time Through a Little Bit of Pre-Design

Being original is an important aspect of your design abilities. Being done is a more important expression of your desire to keep your "high-paying" job. What's a well-intentioned broadcast designer to do? Both!

By creating your own templates based on your designs and styles (or at least those approved by the art director), you can make deadlines and keep the look you want. The word template has gotten a bad stigma thanks to those who think buying a $399 DVD bundle replaces the need for real designers. But you can do good work and save time simultaneously. Let's learn how!

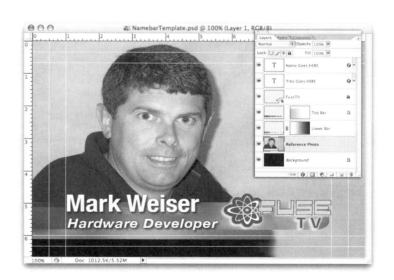

Organization = Success (Photoshop)

When building templates it is critical that the elements of your image are organized. The contents of any template are items that you want to edit, and items that you want to stay the same, so organizing them in with this in mind will keep your templates clean when other people need to use them.

- Separate the editable portions of your template from the fixed elements by placing them into respective layer groups.

- Lock the groups and layers within the groups that you don't want edited or changed.

- Clearly label the groups so that everyone is clear what should be edited and what should be left alone.

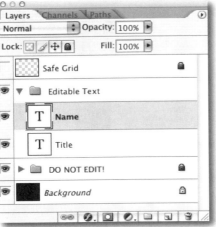

Organization = Success (After Effects)

As with Photoshop, you want to create an organization method in After Effects to keep the editable and fixed elements of your templates separate.

- Use nested comps to separate the elements of a template. We recommend using three comps for templates:

  One for your template elements that you don't want edited

  One for your editable content such as text or pictures

  A render comp that the previous two comps are layered in.

- Name your comps so that they are clearly distinguishable as to what is to be left alone and what can be edited.

- For added protection, lock the layers in the template comps that you don't want moved or edited.

Naming Text Layers

Have you ever noticed that when you create a text layer in Photoshop that the name of the layer assumes the text that was typed into the layer? For the most part this is helpful in identifying layers. However, when working with templates where you have fixed text fields, it is better for your workflow to name the text layers a more descriptive name. For example, if you are creating a lower third template it would be more informative to have a layer labeled "Name" as opposed to the persons name and a layer named "Title" as opposed to the person's title. You can override Photoshop's naming system by changing the name of a layer to a custom name.

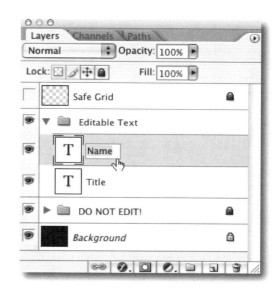

❶ Double click on the name of a text layer.

❷ You will see the name highlight.

❸ Type a new, more descriptive name in for the layer.

❹ Hit the Enter key to accept.

Now the name of the layer will not change as the text within the text layer changes.

Check Your Alignment

When creating templates, the goal of the template should be to make creating a new graphic from the template as easy as possible. When creating your text layers for your graphics, make sure to check the alignment of the text in the Text Tool's options palette when creating the text.

During the design phase of the template is when you should deal with alignment issues. Once the template is done, people should be able to double click on your text layer, type in new text, and not have to worry about whether or not the text aligns properly in the graphic.

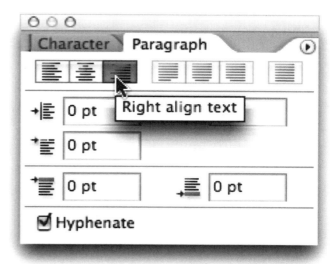

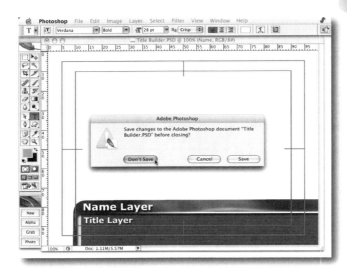

For Once, Don't Save

Another good practice when working with templates is to prevent changes from being made to the template so that other people using the template don't have to worry about things being out of place. Get in the habit of not saving changes to the template when text or other elements are changed for a new version of the image. Save a copy of the template and work from it, or duplicate the file before opening it in Photoshop. This keeps the template in its original state and prevents unwanted accidental changes.

On the Mac OS, you can go one step further.

1 At the Finder level, select the document's icon.

2 Press Cmd+I (Ctr+I) to call up the Info window.

3 Click the Stationary Pad box to use this as a template file. When opened, you will have an untitled copy of the original. This can be edited and saved, but the original file remains untouched.

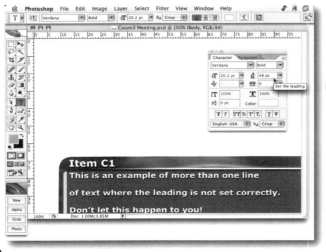

Check Your Leading and Plan Ahead

Keep in mind when designing a template in Photoshop that there may be instances where more than one line of text will be necessary for a given text layer. When designing the template, always type more than 1 line of text into the layers in your templates to make sure that you have the leading set for the layer where you want it. Otherwise you will find that people need to make core changes to the text layers in the template to get line spacing working after the fact.

Don't Overlook Anything

The design phase of the template is where you need to specify fonts and colors for your text layers. When the template is done, all of the text elements need to be set the way you want all graphics that are built from this template to look. Here are a few things to consider and when designing templates.

- Font choice. Save the template with the fonts that you intend to use in the graphics made from the template.

- Text color. Same thing goes for color. Set the text color to the color scheme that you will use in the finished graphics.

- Make sure you use layer styles for text. This makes your text editable so that your text effects follow text changes.

- Check all of your text settings including leading, kerning, tracking and scale.

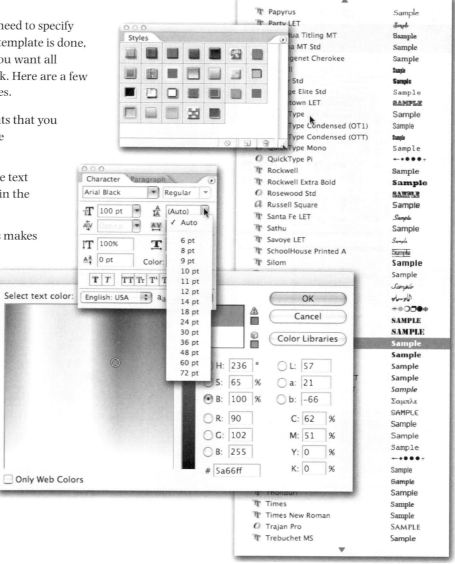

Defining Data Set Variable

Photoshop CS2 has included a new feature called Data Sets. This feature allows you to create a set of data that applies different text to the text layers, different visibility settings to all layers, or pixel replacement for art layers in your document. This is a great feature for use with templates. You can create a template file, then apply data sets to that template and save out individual variations of the template file as individual files. Let's first look at how you define the data set.

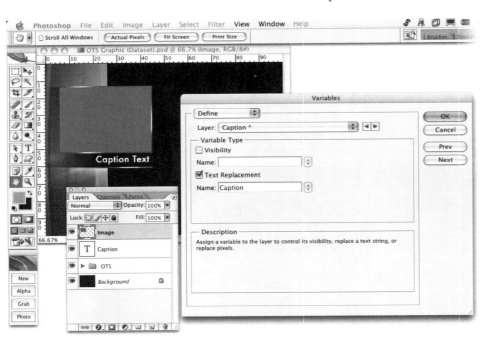

❶ Open the Variables dialog (Image> Variables>Define).

❷ Choose the layer that you want to vary from set to set.

❸ Check the variable types that you wish to control for that layer. Either choose Text Replacement, Pixel Replacement, and/or Visibility.

❹ Assign a name to the variable. This will be used to identify the variable later when sets are created.

❺ Repeat the process for the other layers that need to be varied from one file to the next. Notice that layers that have variables assigned to them have an asterisk next to the layer name.

Now you have defined your variables, look at the next tip to assign data to your variables.

Defining Your Data Sets

Once you have defined your variables, you can create data sets. Each data set corresponds to a variation of your template. For each variable that you created in the previous tip, you can now set values to those variables.

1 Open the Data Set dialog window (Image>Variable>Data Sets).

2 Click the new data set button. This data set is based on the current state of your document.

3 Assign a name to this data set.

4 Move through your variables in the variables list and change the settings for each variable to reflect the state you want your image to be in for this data set.

5 Continue creating new data sets, one for each file variation that you want from your template.

Make Your Data Sets Sing

Once you have created your data set, you can now apply data sets to your template. There are 2 ways to get use your data sets.

1 You can apply an individual data set to your template. Choose Image>Apply Data Set... This will bring up a dialog listing all of the data sets that you created. Choose one and it is applied to your template. At this point, no files have been saved, you are just previewing the template with new variables applied.

2 You can create a new file from the template for each data set that you have created. Choose File>Export>Data Sets as Files. This will bring up a dialog that will allow you to choose the set you want to apply, along with the naming of the files and the location that you want them saved.

One thing to remember about data sets is that they are saved with the file that they are created for. You can not reuse data sets from one template file to another.

External Data Sets

Sure. You can create a text file that can be imported as a data set. This gives you the ability to save your data sets and use them in more than one template file. Here are considerations when creating your data set as a text file for importing.

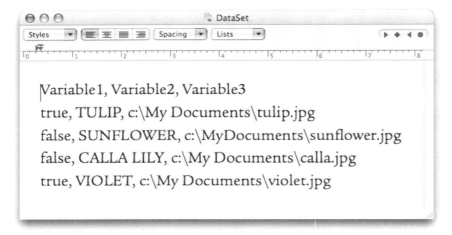

- The first line of the text file needs to be the variables separated by either a comma or a tab.

- The rest of the lines correspond to data sets. Type the setting for each variable separated by either a comma or a tab.

- For Visibility variables, use either "true" or "false."

- For Pixel Replacement variables, type the actual path to the file that you wish to use.

- For Text Replacement variables, simply type the text that you want to use. If your text needs to be in quotes, use double quotes.

Here is a sample:

Variable1, Variable2, Variable3

true, TULIP, c:\My Documents\tulip.jpg

false, SUNFLOWER, c:\MyDocuments\sunflower.jpg

false, CALLA LILY, c:\My Documents\calla.jpg

true, VIOLET, c:\My Documents\violet.jpg

Third-party Template Tools

Tools for Television PRO has a feature called Title Builder, which allows you to replace the text in up to five text layers, and generate individual files for each variation. It also handles the naming of files and creation of alpha channels for each file variation. It is geared towards lower third and factoid graphic creation. Your data sets within Title Builder can be saved out and re-used over multiple template files. For more information and a demo, check it out at http://www. toolsfortelevision.com.

Variety Is the Spice of Life

When creating templates, it is a good idea to create different variations on a theme. For example, you may have more than one full screen template based on the type of content needed for a given graphic. Some graphics may be very text heavy, and others may rely on images or bullet points. We recommend creating multiple variations of a template to fit the different needs that you have. This keeps you working fast and not doing a redesign when it comes time kick out graphics that have unique content. Also consider creating different variations of color schemes for a given template. All of these variations and forethought on your part will save hours down the road in pressure situations.

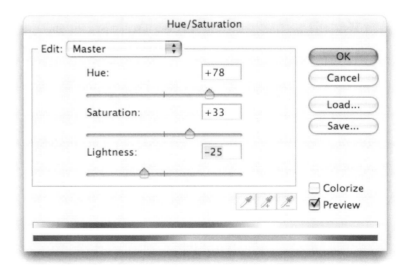

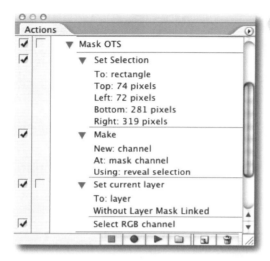

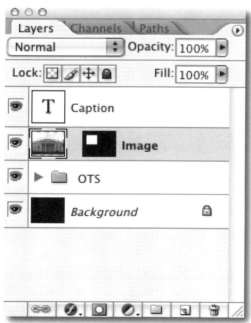

Using Actions with Templates

Many times we will work with templates that incorporate photos or images within the template. And most of the time, such as with an OTS graphic, you want the image to sit within a defined area. You can make bringing new photos into a template very easy by creating an action that applies a layer mask to the photos that masks the image to the pre-defined area. Follow these steps to create the action.

❶ Select the layer that you want to mask.

❷ Create a new action

❸ Make a selection with a marquee tool that fits the pre-defined area that the image needs to be bound by.

❹ Click the add layer mask button.

❺ Unlock the mask from the pixels of the layer.

❻ Stop the action.

Putting it to use:

You now have an action that will mask new elements in the template for you automatically.

❶ Now all you need to do when creating new graphics from the template is to place the photo on a layer inside the template.

❷ Run the action to mask it.

❸ Position the pixels of the layer and transform the size so you are viewing the portion of the photo that you want to see.

Travel with Your Fonts

As important as it is to make sure that your templates are set up with the correct fonts, colors, and other text settings, it is equally important to make sure that when you share your templates between different computers you need to send the fonts that you used with them. Fonts in Photoshop are not embedded in the file and need to be installed on all computers that will use the template.

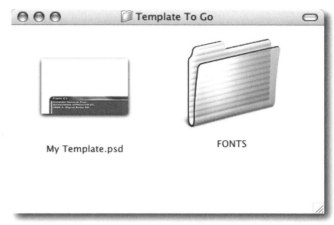

Storing Logos in Photoshop

Did you know that you could save your logos as custom shapes or brushes in Photoshop? This makes it very easy to incorporate them into your templates.

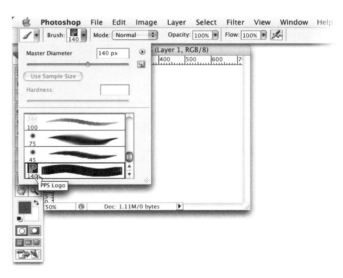

- If you have your logo in the paths palette or as a vector layer, you can select the path and select Edit>Define custom shape. This will save it in the custom shapes tool.

- If your logo is rasterized as pixels, you can create a selection around the outside of the logo and define it as a custom brush (Edit>Define Brush Preset). You can now select the brush tool and paint your logo right onto your template.

Keep in mind that this limits you to using the logo as grayscale, but the foreground and background color selected in Photoshop will tint it when it is applied to a layer.

ON THE SPOT

Logos & Motion
Designing Still and Animated Logos for Video

These days just about every station—heck, just about every program—puts a semi-transparent logo bug in a corner of the screen. It's really no wonder. Photoshop makes this easy enough for anyone to do. And while a nice static bug can be effective, you may want to kick things into a higher gear and actually animate a logo.

Even though a logo may start static, it's not hard to add some life. Prep some layers, give them clear names, and bring them into After Effects for a little motion perhaps. Whatever the method, you'll likely be putting a client's brand on the screen quite often. In this chapter we'll take a look at some easy ways to do that.

Starting Points

Work with a vector logo if possible. Its mathematically defined points allow it to be scaled infinitely without distortion. Pixel based bitmap images look terrible when scaled too high. Photoshop will create and edit vector shapes with some limitations, but even a tiny vector logo can be rescaled to large sizes without losing quality using the Open command's Rasterize options dialog. Even better, if using File>Place under CS2, you'll retain the vector data for future transformations.

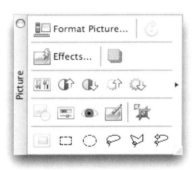

"Worst Logo Format... Ever"

It's happened to all of us... we need a logo, but the only format anyone can find is the logo created (or embedded) inside of Microsoft Word. The trick is to size the logo inside of Word, then send it out.

❶ Open the Microsoft Word document.

❷ Copy the logo to your clipboard.

❸ Create a New document.

❹ Paste the logo.

❺ Click on the logo. The WordArt formatting palette should appear.

❻ Click on the format WordArt button to access scale controls. You should be able to enlarge the logo to the required size. Be sure to click the lock aspect ratio check box. For best results scale it 200% or 400%.

❼ Copy the item to your clipboard. Word works at 300 dpi, so this should provide plenty of pixels to work with.

❽ Create a new document in Photoshop. The new document will automatically be sized to the clipboard's contents.

❾ Paste, save, and start working.

Logos and Fonts

If you need to open a vector logo, be prepared for some problems with your fonts. If the logo designer left the type "live" you're going to need to have the font loaded. Sounds like no big deal, until you realize that some fonts are expensive and others proprietary. The solution, if possible, is to ask the logo designer to convert the type to outlines, and re-save as an EPS or Adobe Illustrator file.

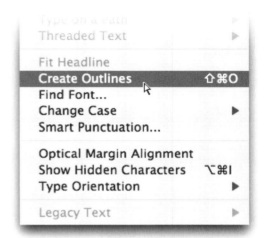

Take the Edge Off

Nothing looks lower-budget than a shapely logo (other than rectangular or square) with a rectangular box of white around it. This "throwaway" border is easy to remove with an alpha channel, and it makes a world of difference. Smaller market stations put graphics with these edges on-air all the time, and it's a shame because fixing it is so simple.

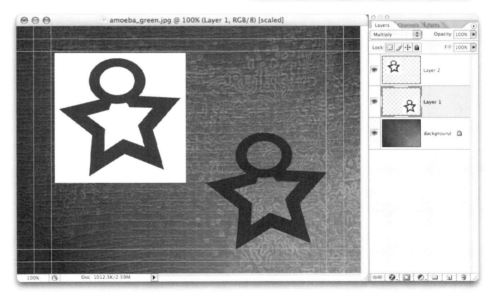

❶ Open the image in Photoshop.

❷ Select the 'throwaway' edges or borders (hold Shift to make multiple selections).

❸ Invert the selection (Select>Inverse).

❹ In the Channels Palette click Save Selection as Channel. You can use a Levels adjustment (and a slight blur if needed) to refine the alpha channel.

❺ Save in a format that preserves alpha channels.

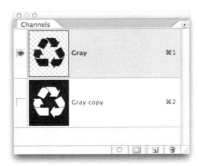

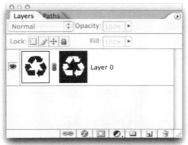

It's Black and White

Got a solid black logo on a solid white background? It's easy to get it off the background.

❶ Convert the logo to grayscale.

❷ Switch to the Channels palette and duplicate the gray channel.

❸ Select the new channel and invert it by pressing Cmd+I (Ctrl+I).

❹ Load the new channel by Cmd+Clicking (Ctrl+Clicking) on its icon.

❺ Disable the new channel.

❻ Switch back to the Layers palette. Make sure the logo is on a floating layer. If it is a locked or background layer, you'll have to double-click and give it a name.

❼ Click on the layer's thumbnail and click on the Apply Layer Mask icon.

Dissolve It All

Seeing through your logo? When you place a logo over a background image or video and add a fade to black to both tracks, the logo dissolves along with the background. While they may fade at the exact same rate, the logo appears to fade faster, showing the background behind it. To avoid this, you have two options:

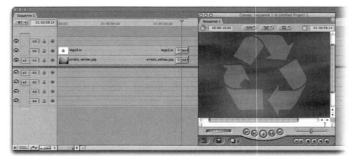

- You can mix the video down with the logo to a pre-rendered track. Then add the fade to black or dissolve to the video / logo composite track. This way you'll get a clean dissolve on the entire screen.

- Place a black solid, slug, or video clip above the track and dissolve up to a higher track.

Your NLE is the Boss

Some NLEs and compositing programs now support
Photoshop's native transparency in PSD files. Programs
like Sony Digital Picture's Vegas, Apple Final Cut Pro, Avid
NLEs, Boris RED, and After Effects will read transparency
without the need for alpha channels and even correctly
interpret Layer Effects like bevels and drop shadows (as long
as you import without layers.) Experiment to see how your
application interprets PSD files.

We Need an Interpreter!

If it can't read your alpha channel, After Effects will prompt you
for interpretation. You can tell it whether you have a straight or
premultiplied alpha, to guess as to which it is (it's often correct), or
even to invert or ignore the channel.

If you want to change your mind, you can reopen the Interpret
dialog by contextual-clicking the item in the Project window
and selecting Interpret Footage. By the way, Photoshop files are
premultiplied with white if you saved them over a transparency
grid; otherwise they are premultiplied with whatever color you
stored in the background layer (such as black).

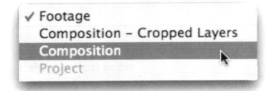

Composite a Composition

Import a multi-layered logo into After Effects as Footage and you'll get a single layer. To maximize your animation capability, import it as a Composition.

❶ Choose File>Import>File.

❷ Navigate to your multi-layered document and select it.

❸ In the Import As box, select Composition. If you choose cropped layers, the anchor points will be at the center of each object. Be aware though that some older filters will be clipped by the bounding box.

Make that Logo Dance

Need to get your logo elements synchronized with music? Wouldn't it be nice to see your beats? This is our favorite way to sync keyframes to your audio track. If you can tap your finger to the music, you can achieve better keyframing.

❶ Add a Solid Layer to Hold your Keyframes by Pressing Cmd+Y (Ctrl+Y). Leave this layer selected.

❷ Set your preview area for the segment of audio you'd like to keyframe.

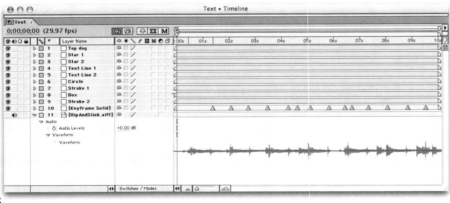

❸ Be certain the Audio button is highlighted in the Time Controls Window.

❹ Start the RAM preview.

❺ To add a Layer Marker, press the Multiply symbol (*) on the numeric keypad. Continue to tape out each audio event you'd like to sync tap.

❻ When the Preview is finished, all of the Layer Markers will appear.

❼ To move between markers use the J and K keys to move left or right respectively.

Legalese

When working with a scanned logo, you may often notice that its legal symbol becomes illegible. You may choose to insert these special characters using the Key Caps on a Mac or the Character Map on a PC. The following keyboard shortcuts are also available on a Mac:

- ™ (Option+2)

- © (Option+G)

- ® (Option+R)

It All Turns Out in the End

Need to animate a logo? (Hey you're in the right chapter!) Here's a simple technique we call slingshot.

1 Go to the end of your imported layers in After Effects, or choose a point where everything should "settle down."

2 View all of the properties you plan to animate. You can press A for Anchor Point, S for Scale, P for Position, R for Rotation, or T for Opacity. Add the shift key to the letter to stack multiple properties.

3 It is a good idea to add the end keyframes first before moving layers. This way, all of the elements will return into proper registration. Turn on the stop watches for each property as needed. You can click on the first stop watch and just drag straight down while keeping the mouse button held down.

4 Grab and move the individual pieces. When you RAM Preview, you'll see everything returns to the right place and remains in perfect registration.

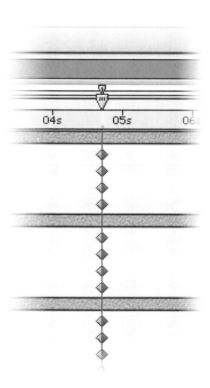

Prepping an AI for Animation

Logos animate much better when you've got them split into pieces. If you're using Adobe Illustrator, an Illustrator or vector EPS file can be easily split into layers. These layers can then be saved out into a layered Photoshop file, which can be tweaked in Photoshop and easily imported into After Effects. Alternately you can import a layered vector file directly into After Effects. Once there, you can animate and render. See? That's only six degrees of separation. Let's try it out.

1 Open a vector logo in Adobe Illustrator.

2 Call up the layer's palette and flip down the twirl-down menu. You should see every item in the logo listed separately.

3 It is necessary to consolidate items a bit to make them more manageable. Press A to activate the Direct Selection tool. Lasso around items that you'd like to keep together and choose Object>Group or press Cmd+G (Ctrl+G).

4 Go to the palette's submenu and choose Release to Layers (Sequence). This will put each group on a new layer.

5 If you would like to name a layer, double-click on its name. You can also drag the layers to change their stacking order. For predictable results, it is a good idea to "un-nest" the layers by dragging them out of the layer set.

6 Choose File>Export; then name the file and select Photoshop (.psd) as the format.

7 Specify resolution, and choose to write layers. Do not change the color model during export. It may affect the on-screen appearance (especially with gradients and transparency). Allow Photoshop to do your color conversions instead.

8 Open up the file in Photoshop. All your layers should be intact. Feel free to filter or process the image with layer styles (if you use styles, be sure to flatten them by merging the stylized layer with an empty layer).

9 Import into your editing or compositing application.

Gentle Moves

Instead of slamming on the brakes with your moves... try a gentler stopping technique.
Select your keyframes and try a little bit of ease:

❶ Click on the keyframe you'd like to apply ease to.

❷ Choose Animation>Keyframe Assistant> and choose one of the following:

- Easy Ease – Gently move both into and out of the keyframe

- Easy Ease In – Slowly move into the keyframe, coming to a gradual stop.

- Easy Ease Out – Apply inertia to the movement out from the keyframe.

Looking for a shortcut? Here's three!

- Easy Ease   F9

- Easy Ease In   Shift+F9

- Easy Ease Out   Cmd+Shift+F9 (Ctrl+Shift+F9)

Sound Keys: For Serious Audio Work

Animated logos are frequently tied to sound. If you are looking for an easy way to get your logo elements synced (such as the words pulsing to the kickdrum) you should take a close look at Trapcode's Sound Keys. While the interface may seem intimidating at first, you'll quickly discover that is allows you to generate keyframes based on specific audio frequencies, This is useful when you want to use the bass to trigger one animation, and the midtones to affect another property. Full details and plenty of documentation can be found at www.trapcode.com.

179

3D Assistants for Exploding Layers

The lite version of 3D assistants from Digital Anarchy comes on your AE install disc. We can use these to create animated logos in a jiffy. Using the Cubic Distribution assistants you can have a bunch of layers start off in random directions, then move into place.

❶ Import your logo as a layered composition.

❷ Promote all of the layers to 3D by clicking on the cube-shaped icon.

❸ Add keyframes towards the end of your comp for position, rotation, anchor point, scale, orientation and opacity (yes.. we call this "idiot keyframing"... better safe then sorry).

❹ Move your current time indicator to the front of the composition.

❺ Select all 3D layers and choose Window>Cubic Distribution Lite.

❻ Set the Cube Dimensions to 3000 pixels by 3000 pixels by 3000 pixels. Before you click apply, though... Select 'Random' under the Layer Orientation options and turn on Set Keys for Position and Orientation. You'll want the Cubic Distribution assistant to set keyframes for all the layers so that they animate when their position and rotation change.

❼ Now... click Apply. The layers are thrown apart in 3D space.

❽ Click RAM Preview to see the movement. Modify keyframes to taste.

Ray to the Rescue

Need a simple logo animation that looks good and takes very little time (okay we admit... that's dumb even for a rhetorical question). Starting with AE 6.5, you'll find the Cycore Effects bundled on the install disk (you have to manually run the installer). One of the coolest effects in the bunch is the CC Light Wipe.

1 Split your logo into separate elements.

2 To each piece, choose Effect>Transition>CC Light Wipe. You may want to stagger the start times.

3 Set keyframes for transition complete. You will want to go from 100% to 0% to reveal the logo. You may want to click the Reverse Transition box.

4 Modify the Center points to taste.

5 Check the Color from Source Box for most realistic results, or pick a wipe color and adjust the Intensity to taste.

6 Adjust the shape to be Round, Square, or Doors.

7 If the bounding box is chopping the effect at the edges, then click the Continuously Rasterize box.

8 RAM Preview the results, adjust the keyframe locations in the Timeline to stagger the effect.

9 When rendering, choose a straight alpha for the cleanest key in your editing or keying application.

ON THE SPOT

CHAPTER 13

OTS Workshop
Creating Over The Shoulder Graphics Faster

It's one of the most important elements in a newscast. It reinforces, explains, or somehow drives the message your news anchor is trying to communicate (or sometimes just fills a "hole" when no video is ready.) The over-the-shoulder (OTS) graphic is standard stuff for just about every TV newscast.

In this chapter we'll cover how to make a fully customizable, easily changed OTS graphic for your newscast. Along the way we'll outline how these concepts also apply to lower-third elements as well.

image courtesy http://tour.diabetes.org

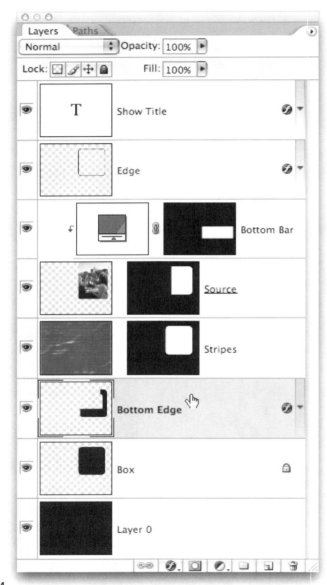

Step Up to the Template

News production is a quick business. You've got deadlines, so you need to implement the quickest and most efficient process possible for making OTS graphics. Building a template to work with allows you (and other producers) to avoid reinventing the wheel, while also ensuring the show's continuity isn't compromised.

To make a template:

1 Sketch or envision a design that will work with your newscast. Be sure to follow any font, color, or style guide standards for your environment.

2 Create a new document using the preset size for your particular NLE or tape format.

3 Design the OTS graphic template using as many layers as needed. Avoid flattening or merging elements when possible. Use of layer masks or clipping masks will allow for a flexible design that is easy to change.

4 Define the alpha channel, often this won't change from one OTS to another. If using Photoshop CS2, be sure to check out the Create Alpha Channel from Visible Layers action which can be found in the new Video Actions preset.

5 Save the template as a PSD for further editing, preferably to a network drive. At the Finder or Desktop Level, lock the file so future versions have to be saved with a new name. This will preserve your template for future projects.

With the template on a network drive, multiple producers can access the document, quickly use the Save As command to save a copy of it before making changes, and proceed.

Examining an Example, Part 1

Create an example by following these steps. When we're done, we'll have a working OTS graphic template.

1 Create a new document by selecting File>New.

2 Choose the NTSC D1 720 x 486 (with guides) preset. Make sure the Color Mode is set to RGB and click OK.

3 Your new document opens with action and title safe guides.

4 With the Rounded Rectangle tool, drag from where the title safe guides meet in an upper corner to just under halfway down the image and just under halfway across the image. (Imagine your anchor sitting in the image and draw where you think the OTS image should be.)

5 Cmd+click (Ctrl+click) the shape layer to select it.

6 Switch to the Channels Palette and click Save Selection as Channel.

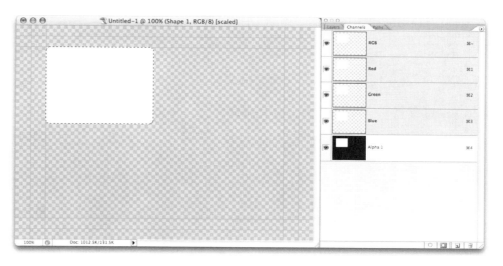

7 Click the visibility indicator on the new alpha channel.

8 Save the file in a format that preserves alpha channels and that your NLE will read.

You've just create a very basic OTS template. The rounded rectangle shape represents the image that will appear over your anchor's shoulder. Since there is an alpha channel defining transparency around everything except this shape (where you see color overlay), this shape represents is the only place images will show through. Everything else will be masked.

Examining an Example, Part 2

Now that we've got a simple template, let's prep it. For this example, let's assume you have a frame grab from the story you're making the OTS for.

❶ Open the template and your frame grab. If you haven't done so already, be sure to run the De-Interlace filter on your frame grab (Filter>Video>De-Interlace...) Otherwise, the interlacing will be a problem when you scale the image.

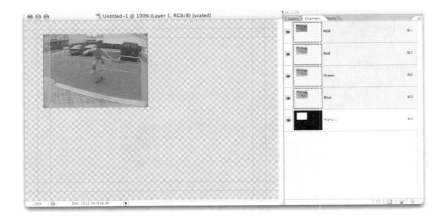

❷ Using the Move tool, drag the frame grab into the template.

❸ If it's not on, turn the alpha channel's visibility on by switching to the Channels Palette and clicking its visibility icon.

❹ Click the frame grab layer to activate it.

❺ Press Cmd+T (Ctrl+T) to transform the image. Holding down Shift+Option (Shift+Alt) will allow you to scale the image towards the center while constraining proportions.

❻ Resize so that the portion of the image you want to see over the anchor's shoulder is not obstructed by the color overlay.

❼ Press Return (Enter) to accept the transformation

Now your image will appear over the anchor's shoulder. Remember, anything under the alpha channel (represented by the color overlay), will not show through. You don't need to erase or mask it in any other way. The alpha channel will take care of it.

If you're the kind of person who likes to see what it's going to look like while still in Photoshop, use a Clipping Mask.

❶ Place the frame grab immediately above the shape layer.

❷ Choose Layer>Create Clipping Mask (or Group with Previous depending on your version) to mask the image to your shape.

Working Outside the Box

Now that you've got a frame grab in the OTS template, you'll probably want to add some text. A one or two word "slug" is common for OTS graphics. For this example, assume we want the text to be just underneath the box. Because it will sit under the alpha channel, we will have to adjust that to make sure it will be visible.

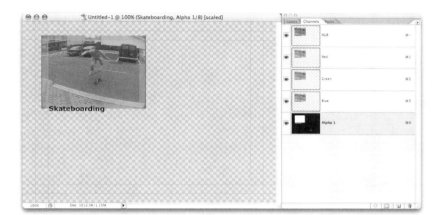

1 With the Type tool, type a one or two-word slug under the image, just outside the box.

2 Use the Move tool to position it in an appropriate place.

3 Load the type as a selection by Cmd+clicking (Ctrl+clicking) the type layer.

4 Switch to the Channels palette.

5 Click the alpha channel.

6 Press Delete (Backspace) to remove the alpha channel from the selected area over the text

Keep in mind that we only had to delete the alpha channel because we put the text outside the shape where the alpha would mask it. Using this template method you can save multi-layered files for reuse or further editing.

Sticky Notes

Want to put some comments into your template? Then use the Notes Tool (N). Once selected, you can click inside of your document to add comments for the next designer (or yourself before coffee).

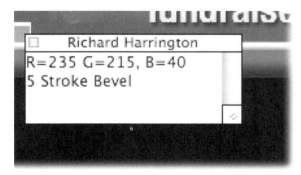

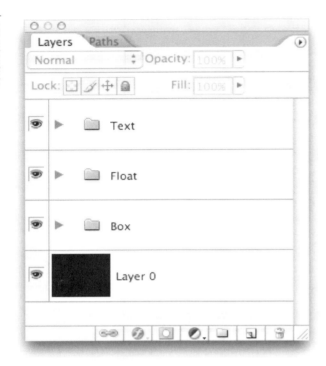

Consider Being Considerate

So far our template has been very simple. We have not added any image compositing or layer effects, but you can imagine how we could easily end up with several layers. The whole idea of using a template is to keep things orderly (for continuity) and simple, so it only makes sense to rename layers out of consideration for whomever might need to use that same file a few months later... you never know; it might be you!

❶ To rename a layer, double click its name in the Layers palette and type a new name.

❷ Use descriptive names so users can identify layers at a glance (remember, the idea is to make this quick and easy)!

To organize really complex documents, consider putting similar elements into layer groups (or sets).)

❶ Under CS2, select multiple layers by Cmd+Clicking, Ctrl+Clicking. In earlier versions, click the link icon in the layers palette.

❷ Press Cmd+G (Ctrl+G) in CS2. Otherwise select New Group from Layers (or New Set From Linked) from the Layers Palette sub menu.

Left...No Right

For flexibility during the live show, you will need to send your graphic in so it is able to be keyed over the left and right shoulder. Does this mean twice as much work? Nope.

❶ Turn off the visibility for all layers (including the background) that should not be in the final graphic.

❷ Choose Select>All or press Cmd+A (Ctrl+A).

❸. Copy all layers to your clipboard by choosing Edit>Copy Merged or pressing Shift+Cmd+C (Shift+Ctrl+C)

❹. Paste a copy into your document.

❺ Using guides (or Smart Guides in CS2) align the image with its counterpart.

The Awesome (Gradient) Editor

Gradients make for excellent background graphic elements. Photoshop's Gradient Editor allows you to browse the available gradient presets.

❶ Select the Gradient tool (G) from the toolbox.

❷ Several settings become available in the Options bar.

❸ Click on the preview of the gradient in the Option bar to open the Gradient Editor.

❹ The Editor opens and displays available presets. You can open more gradient presets by selecting one of the categories at the bottom of the sub menu.

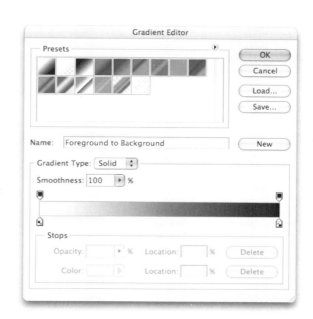

Gradient Screen Graphics

Some news programs use a different kind of OTS graphic. This style of graphic runs from the top of the screen down to the bottom, gradually fading out over the anchor. This type of graphic employs a gradient alpha channel.

❶ Open a background image.

❷ In the Channels Palette, click the Create New Channel button.

❸ A new alpha channel is created, masking the image fully by default.

❹ Select the visibility indicator of the RGB track in the Channels Palette, then select the alpha channel.

❺ Using the Gradient tool and the default colors of black to white, draw a straight line where you want the background to fade out. Make sure to drag from the inside of the image toward the outside. Hold Shift while dragging to keep the gradient perfectly straight.

❻ The color overlay changes, revealing your new gradient alpha channel.

❼ Save the file in a format that preserves alpha channels (such as PICT or TARGA) and that your NLE, still store, or CG will read.

But Wait, There's More!

The top half of the Gradient Editor deals with presets. The bottom half displays the current gradient and allows you to adjust it and save it to create your own custom gradients. Here's how it works.

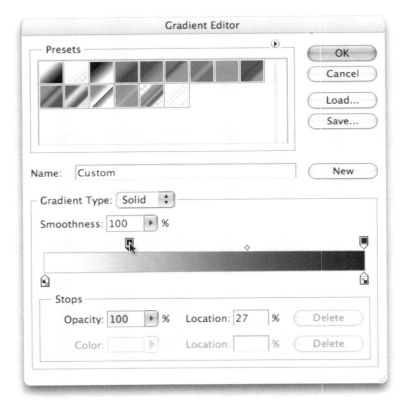

- The gradient is flanked with boxed arrows called Stops.

- Stops on top of the gradient represent opacity. To change their value, click on the stop. The Opacity setting become active, allowing you to change it.

- Once you alter an Opacity Stop, a small diamond appears representing the midpoint. This changes the interpolation of the gradient's opacity.

- The boxed arrows under the gradient are Color Stops. To change the color of the gradient, click a stop and change the color in the Color setting or double click the stop to bring up a color palette.

- Click between two color stops to add an additional color.

- Click along the top of the gradient to add a new Opacity Stop and below it to create a new Color Stop.

- Click and drag a stop to move it. Click and choose Delete get rid of a stop (or drag it up or down). The gradient updates to show you what a fill will look like.

- For a different look, switch the Gradient Type to Noise and experiment by limiting modifying the Color Model. Click the Randomize button for new options.

- Enter a new name and choose New to save your custom gradient.

- It appears in the Presets window.

Live Layers

Need to make quick changes to your OTS frame or gradients? Then try using Fill Layers instead of your Gradient and Paint Bucket Tools.

① Create an active selection by either loading a layer or using a selection tool.

② Choose Layer>New Fill Layer> Gradient or Solid Color

③ In the dialog box, you'll have a standard color picker or gradient editor...edit to taste.

④ Click OK.

⑤ When you need to make a last minute change (or the producer gets picky) just double-click the layer's thumbnail to invoke the editor. This is a VERY fast way to make little tweaks as you won't need to keep loading gradients or swatches and making new selections.

Detach those Masks

Using Layer Masks in your design? In the case of templates, it much more useful if the mask stays put, but the fill can be moved.

① If you click on the chain icon between the layer and mask thumbnails, they are no longer linked.

② Now you can select either the fill or the matte by clicking on their thumbnails (you'll see a small border around the icon).

③ Using the move tool, you can nudge things into place.

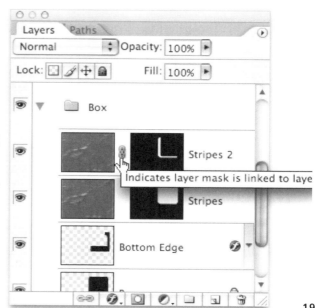

Put the Concept to Work

You can apply something similar to the OTS method we used to create lower thirds for your programs. Lower thirds are commonly used as backdrops for titles, used to identify people in interviews, for example. When a reporter comes on screen, a lower third pops (or fades) up so the viewer can see the reporter's name, commonly along with a program or network logo.

Lower thirds can simply be background images with alpha channels set to mask parts of the image. Creating one is easy.

1 Open a background image in Photoshop.

2 In the Channels Palette, click the Create New Channel button.

3 A new alpha is created, masking the image fully by default.

4 Select the visibility indicator of the RGB track in the Channels Palette, then select the alpha channel.

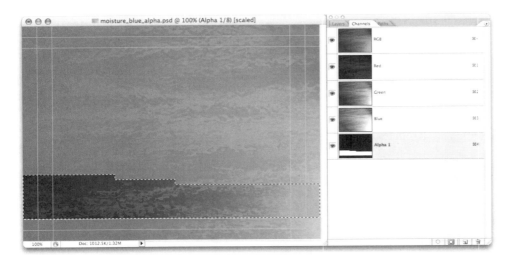

5 Using a selection tool, create a selection that includes the area where you'd like the lower third to appear in the image. It can be as simple or as complex as you like.

6 Using the Brush tool, paint these selected areas white.

7 The color overlay disappears where you paint white, which indicates that pixels in that part of the image will be visible.

8 Use the Type tool to create text identifying your reporter, etc.

Distinguishing Speakers

Lower thirds often include two lines of text, one for the name of the person speaking and one for his or her title (although we've seen an out-of-control producer try to use four lines once). You can include a separation line between them, a simple but effective way to distinguish the two bits of information.

1 Add two lines of text to your lower third: one for the person's name and one for their title. Generally, the person's name is set in a larger font (as well as an alternate style or face) since it's often shorter than his or her title.

2 Using the Rectangle or Rounder Rectangle tool, draw a thin box between the top and bottom lines of text.

3 Alternately, use the Rectangular Marquee tool to draw the line and fill it with a solid color or gradient.

4 Finally, you can add your station or program's logo to the lower third to complete the effect.

ON THE SPOT

CHAPTER 14

Effect Essentials
Some Effects to Spark Your Creativity

While effects should only be used as a spice to good design, they still can be fun and essential to the overall project. Effects can catch your audience's eye as well as set you apart from the competition.

In this chapter we unlock several popular looks using built-in tools. These techniques are all fast and you should be able to record them as actions or animation presets. Be sure to not stop here, the techniques used in these effects can be easily modified into new and exciting looks as well. Jump into the effects pool and see how things turn out.

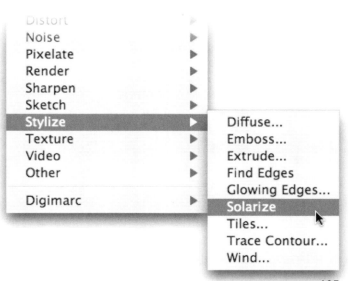

Film Look in After Effects

There are several solutions for achieving a realistic film look... most involve the use of third-party filters. While we believe in and support third-party filters, we thought we'd share a way that uses only built-in tools.

1 Add your clip into a new comp. The easiest way to do this is to drag your shot onto the new comp icon at the bottom of the project window.

2 Duplicate the shot by pressing Cmd+D (Ctrl+D).

3 Apply a blur filter to the top layer. Fast Blur, Gaussian Blur, or Box Blur are all good options. Adjust the blur so it is fairly heavy.

4 With the top layer still selected, press Shift+= to cycle through your blending modes. Different modes may be required due to your original source material. Stop when the saturation and blooming matches your artistic goals. Press Shift+- to move backwards through your blending modes.

5 Choose Layer>New Adjustment Layer.

6 Now add the grain by choosing Effects>Noise & Grain>Add Grain. Adjust the Softness, Intensity, and Size of your grain to taste.

7 Add a Black Solid by choosing Layer>New Solid or pressing Cmd+Y (Ctrl+Y).

8 With the Black Solid selected, switch to the Toolbox and double-click on the Rectangular Mask Tool to make a new mask.

9 Select the mask for the black solid by pressing MM to call up mask properties. Set the following values: Invert (check on), Pixels 35 (adjust to taste), Mask Expansion -10 (adjust to taste).

10 Make the shot broadcast safe by adding a new adjustment layer at the top of your stack, then apply Effect>Video>Broadcast Colors.

Cartoon Look

Need to pull of that cel-animated look? Try this technique on your stills or footage.

In Photoshop

❶ Open and size the image.

❷ Run the Find Edges Filter (Filter>Stylize>Find Edges). There is no dialog box for this effect.

❸ Immediately after running the filter, Fade it by Choosing Edit>Fade Find Edges or pressing Shift+Cmd+F (Shift+Ctrl+F). Remember this shortcut by saying I want to command (or control) how the filter Shifts (i.e. Fades).

❹ Try Overlay mode and adjust the opacity slider to taste. Depending on your source image, you can use different blending modes.

In After Effects

❶ Add your clip into a new comp. The easiest way to do this is to drag your shot onto the new comp icon at the bottom of the project window.

❷ Duplicate the shot by pressing Cmd+D (Ctrl+D).

❸ Apply the Find Edges effect by choosing Effect>Stylize>Find Edges.

❹ Change the blending mode an opacity of the layer. You may also want to add a Fast Blur effect to smooth out your results.

Image courtesy the American Diabetes Association - tour.diabetes.org

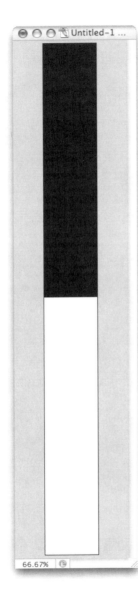

66.67%

Realistic Scan Lines

This effect is a cliché... yet nothing says "high-tech" like some scan lines. As an added bonus... make it green and glowy (like *the Matrix*)... clients love that. No really they do (PLEASE make it stop). But since bad taste won't change your deadline... lets at least learn the fastest way of pulling of this effect.

1 In Photoshop, make a new document that is ten pixels tall and one pixel wide.

2 With the Rectangular Marquee, select the top five pixels.

3 Fill with a color of your choice or black (how boring).

4 Choose Select>Inverse then fill with a second color or white.

5 Choose Select>All.

6 Create a pattern by choosing Edit>Define Pattern. Give the pattern a descriptive name such as scanlines (again, how boring).

7 Create a new document that matches your video frame size.

8 Choose Edit>Fill and select Pattern. Navigate to the pattern you created.

9 Soften the image slightly by blurring it at a low value.

10 Save your Scan Lines as a file for Import into After Effects.

11 Import the scan lines into After Effects and place it over your footage.

⑫ Adjust its blending mode to taste (remember Shift+= is a fast way to experiment). You may want to lower the opacity as well.

⑬ Place an Adjustment Layer on Top and apply a blur such as Effect>Blur>Fast Blur.

⑭ Blend the blurred layer slightly to create a glow. Setting it to Soft Light at 40% Opacity often works well.

If your Keanu-loving client insists, add a second adjustment layer.

⑮ Apply the Colorama effect by choosing Effect>Image Control>Colorama.

⑯ Under the Output Cycle, choose Ramp Green (RGB creates a nice Infrared Effect and Fire can create a nice old-school amber monitor look).

⑰ Change the Colorama layer's blending mode to Hue (or experiment with others).

⑱ Take the red pill (or blue... your choice).

Bad Boy Cop Blur

Often times you'll have someone in your shot that you need to obscure (such as an underage individual or maybe a bystander who you didn't get clearance on). This technique works in both Photoshop and After Effects.

❶ Duplicate your footage or background layer.

❷ Apply the Mosaic effect. In Photoshop, choose Filter>Pixelate>Mosaic... and adjust to taste. In After Effects, choose Effect>Stylize>Mosaic (increase the number of blocks)

❸ Apply a layer mask or vector mask to the top copy around the individual's face on the mosaic layer

❹ Feather your edges on your mask and expand the edges as needed.

❺ If the person moves, you'll need to keyframe the mask in After Effects.

As a side note, cop blurs can be used to help hide cultural differences. For example, take your stereotypical bad gangster rap video. In the US, we're quick to cover up any nudity. The same video at MTV Europe, they're worried about obscuring the guns in the frame. Rich says he likes European thinking much better sometimes.

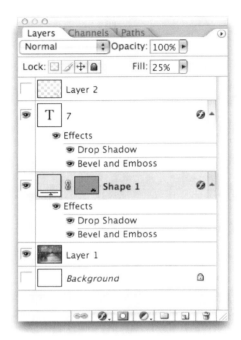

Image courtesy the American Diabetes Association - tour.diabetes.org

Glass Bug

Need to create a network jelly bug? Those semi-transparent logos that sit in the corner and look like they are made from glass?

1 Split your logo or bug up into as many layers as you need so the pieces are clearly separated.

2 Be sure you have transparency in the objects.

3 Place a reference photo or frame grab below the

4 Apply a Bevel and Emboss layer style as well as a slight drop shadow. Keep the Bevel thin and crisp.

5 Adjust the Fill command for the layer, which will lower the original fill, but preserve the opacity of the effects. You can do this from the Blending Options: Custom area of the Styles dialog box or from the top of the Layers palette.

6 Turn off all layers except the bug. If you have Photoshop CS2, run the Alpha Channels from Visible Layers action (part of the Video Actions set. Skip to step 11.

7 Make a new (empty layer) and select it.

8 Choose Layer>Merge Visible while holding down the Option (Alt) key. You will get a merged copy that is perfectly registered with the layers below.

9 Cmd+Click (Ctrl+Click) the new layer's thumbnail in the Layers Palette to load the Selection.

10 Switch to the Channels Palette and click the Save Selection as Channel button to create an Alpha Channel.

11 Save the file as a PICT, Targa, or PNG-24.

12 Import into After Effects or your NLE. You should tell it that the graphic is pre-multiplied with white to get the cleanest edge.

Liquid

A lot of the top motion graphics designs are being done "outside the box." By "the box" we mean your computer. Get out and film or videotape something.

Here's a fast way to create liquid effects from your illustrations:

1. Set up a camera and lights with a card stand or area that is well lit for a piece of paper containing artwork.

2. Print out your artwork and dissolve it while the ink is still wet with rubbing alcohol. While recording, you can pour this on or spray it on and let it get smeared and organic looking. For best results, shoot a progressive frame rate.

3. Capture the footage into your system.

4. Then in After Effects, simply run your footage backwards and you'll have that mess turn back into a beautiful illustration or logo. (Assuming, of course, that your illustration IS beautiful.) Nonetheless, you'll have a cool-looking effect that couldn't have been achieved with filters.

By Jayse Hansen, http://www.xeler8r.com

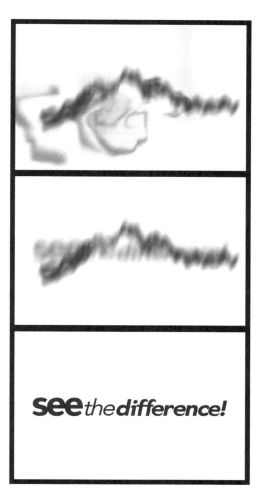

Zoom Lines in Photoshop

This effect produces a nice light blast from the focal point of an object and is a popular advertising look.

1 Duplicate your layer by pressing Cmd+J (Ctrl+J).

2 Desaturate the duplicate layer by pressing Cmd+Shift+U (Ctrl+Shift+U).

3 Apply a Zoom Blur by selecting Filter>Radial Blur>Zoom.

4 Use an amount of 100 at Good quality. Move the center-point by dragging within the dialog box.

5 Specify the maximum blur and position the focal point for the blur at the focal point of your object. Click OK.

6 Repeat the Blur filter by pressing Cmd+F (Ctrl+F).

7 On the top layer, make a Levels adjustment (Image>Adjustments>Levels). Bring the black and white sliders towards center. Move the gray slider, (the midpoint) away from black.

8 Change the blend mode of the layer to taste.

9 Run a levels adjustment on the background to add some additional contrast.

10 Using a soft-edge brush and the eraser tool set to 30 percent opacity, erase away parts of the blast layer, leaving just the image below. This can be useful on areas with detail such as faces or text.

Zoom Lines in After Effects

Need to pull the same zoom effect in After Effects? Here's how.

1. Add your clip into a new comp. The easiest way to do this is to drag your shot onto the new comp icon at the bottom of the project window.

2. Duplicate the shot by pressing Cmd+D (Ctrl+D). Name the layer Rays.

3. Desaturate the duplicate layer by choosing Effect>Image Control>Hue/Saturation. Set the Saturation Slider to -100.

4. Starting with AE 6.5, the Cycore Effects are bundled on your install disc. Choose Effect>Blur>CC Radial Fast Blur. If this is not an option, choose the regular Radial Blur and be prepared to go walk down the street for a cup of coffee. Adjust the Center and Amount of your effect.

5. Adjust your Levels on the Blur Layer by Choosing Effect>Adjust>Levels. Pull your Black and White Input sliders in towards the edges of your Histogram. This will increase the contrast of your layer

6. Experiment with different blending modes and opacities. You may want to adjust the gray slider on the Levels effect to tweak the rays' intensity.

7. To limit the effect, duplicate your original source layer, name it Mask and place it on top. If you have a lot of motion in the shot, you'll need to keyframe a mask and roughly rotoscope the shot with a soft edge. If the shot is fairly static, just double click it to load in the footage window and use your Eraser tool.

8. Change the Track Matte of the Rays layer and set it to Alpha Inverted using the Matte layer.

9. You may want to combine this effect with the previously mentioned Film Look technique to boost saturation.

Images courtesy the American Diabetes Association - tour.diabetes.org

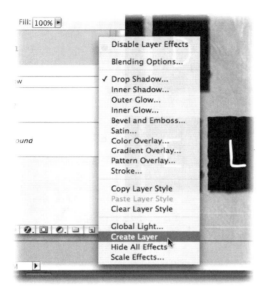

Cast Shadows in Photoshop

A lot of folks we know express frustration at the ability to make believable drop shadows inside of Photoshop. When using layer styles... you get a very tight drop shadow, but it contains no perspective or sense of being cast.

1 Position the logo or element where you want it. It needs to contain transparency and be on its own layer.

2 Duplicate the layer by pressing Cmd+J (Ctrl+J).

3 Press D to load the default colors of black and white.

4 Lock the transparency of the layer by clicking on Lock Transparent Pixels icon at the top of the Layers palette.

5 Fill the selection by pressing Option+Delete (Alt+delete).

6 Apply Free Transform by pressing Cmd+T (Ctrl+T) to the layer and select the Perspective Transformation. Access the perspective distortion by Ctrl+clicking (right-clicking). Be sure to grab the transform handle in the middle of the top edge. Put it to the right or left, depending on your "light" source.

7 Access the scale command by Ctrl+clicking (right-clicking). Adjust the length of the shadow to taste.

8 Click the Apply Transformations box, or press Return (Enter).

9 Blur the shadow and change its blending mode to Multiply.

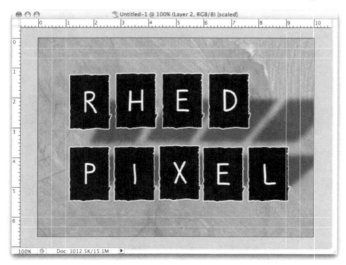

Instant BG – Fractal Noise (After Effects)

Everyone can use motion backgrounds! Here's a technique to make some from scratch within After Effects.

❶ Create a new comp sized for your tape format.

❷ Add a new solid by pressing Cmd+Y (Ctrl+Y).

❸ Choose Effect>Noise & Grain>Fractal Noise.

❹ By default it looks like Photoshop's cloud filters... try switching the fractal type and noise type for dramatic results.

❺ Adjust Contrast, Brightness and Transform properties to taste.

❻ Set a keyframe for evolution at the start and leave it set to 0 (zero). Go to the end of your composition and add a second keyframe. Set this to a whole number if you'd like to create a seamless loop. Be sure to check the Cycle Evolution box under Evolution Options.

❼ If you'd like greater movement, use the Offset Turbulence command under the Transform option. Add two keyframes, one at start and finish. Double-click one of the keyframes to modify it. Switch to Percentage of Composition and change the value from 50 (which is centered) to 150 (which is one full offset cycle).

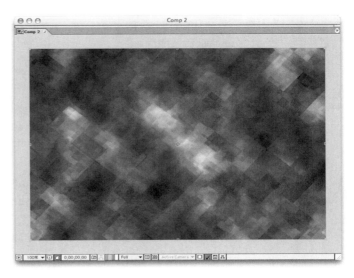

❽ To add some depth, you can duplicate the layer and modify its fractal and noise type. Then blend the two layers.

❾ Add an adjustment layer with a Fast Blur effect applied. Blur heavily and then blend to produce highlights.

❿ Add another adjustment layer with either a Colorama or Tint effect to colorize the layer. Then blend as desired. Be sure to adjust the Output cycle on the Colorama effect.

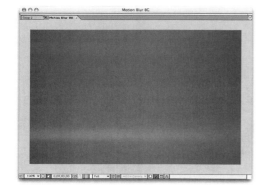

Instant BG – Directional Blur (After Effects)

Need a soft, amorphous background? All you need is some footage, a couple of effects, and some render time.

❶ Create a new comp sized for your tape format and make it 12:00 long.

❷ Add a piece of footage to your composition and trim the ends to match your comp. You can trim the out point by going to the end of your comp and selecting the footage layer. Then press Option+] (Alt+]) to trim the outpoint.

❸ Apply blur effects to your footage. Any of the effects will work, but Directional Blur is particularly nice here.

❹ Go to the middle of your comp, and split your footage layer by pressing Shift+Cmd+D (Shift+Ctrl+D).

❺ Shorten your composition to 10:00 by pressing Cmd+K (Ctrl+K) and typing in the new duration.

❻ Select the top layer and press the Home key. Move the top layer to start at the beginning of the comp (shortcut key [will move the in point to the Current Time Indicator).

❼ Select the bottom layer and press the End key. Move the bottom layer to end at the end of the comp (shortcut key] will move the outpoint to the Current Time Indicator).

❽ Place an Opacity fade between the top and bottom layer.

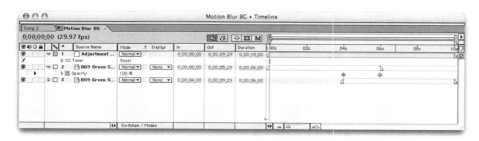

❾ Add Adjustment Layers with additional blurring and colorization effects such as Colorama or CC Toner. Be sure to adjust the Output cycle on the Colorama effect.

This effect works very well on almost all footage. You can easily set up several clips to run overnight in your render queue to build up your backgrounds library.

Instant BG – Wave World (After Effects)

Need a rounded, undulating background? Then check out Wave World (but skip Waterworld... not worth seeing).

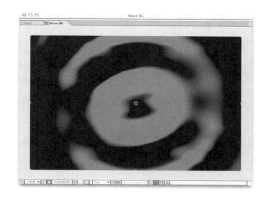

1 Create a new comp sized for your tape format set to 12:00 long.

2 Add a new solid by pressing Cmd+Y (Ctrl+Y).

3 Choose Effect>Simulation>Wave World.

4 Initially, you see a Wireframe Preview. Switch to view the Height Map.

5 Adjust the various controls to taste, there are several options, but they provide quick feedback. Be sure to adjust the pre-roll effect so the waves are in full force at the beginning.

6 Go to the middle of your comp, and split your wave footage layer by pressing Shift+Cmd+D (Shift+Ctrl+D).

7 Select the top wave layer and press the Home key. Move the top layer to start at the beginning of the comp (shortcut key [will move the in point to the Current Time Indicator).

8 Shorten your composition to 10:00 by pressing Cmd+K (Ctrl+K) and typing in the new duration.

9 Select the bottom layer and press the End key. Move the bottom layer to end at the end of the comp (shortcut key] will move the outpoint to the Current Time Indicator).

10 Place an Opacity fade between the top and bottom layer.

11 Add an adjustment layer with a CC Radial Fast Blur effect applied. Blur heavily and then blend to produce highlights.

12 Add Adjustment Layers with additional blurring and colorization effects such as Colorama or CC Toner. Be sure to adjust the Output cycle on the Colorama effect. Then blend as desired.

Write It On (After Effects)

It's pretty easy to get your text and other graphic elements to have that "written on" look. Whether you are using your own hand-drawn graphics, scanned artwork, or computer generated art, the technique is pretty much the same.

❶ Place a new solid above your artwork by pressing Cmd+Y (Ctrl+Y)

❷ Set the solid to 50% opacity so you can see your art below it

❸ Use the pen tool to trace over it. Add as few points as possible, and add them in the order that you would draw the piece on.

❹ Add Effect>Stylize>Write On effect and set it Paint Style to On Transparent.

❺ Select the solid layer and press M and select Mask Shape.

❻ Press Cmd +C (Ctrl+C) to copy the mask.

❼ Press E to reveal the effects on the layer, then twirl down the Write On effect and select Brush Position.

❽ Press Cmd+V (Ctrl+V) to paste the mask position as keyframes

❾ Play the animation to see it draw on. You may need to increase the brush size to see it.

❿ Increase the brush size until it covers your artwork.

⓫ Decrease the Brush spacing to .001.

⓬ Drag the end keyframe to slow the animation or speed it up. You'll notice that the inner keyframes are pasted as roving keyframes so they'll adapt automatically.

⓭ Set your artwork/text layer's track matte as the Alpha Matte of the Write On layer. It should now reveal the layer beneath it.

By Jayse Hansen, http://www.xeler8r.com

Effect Controls panel:

g • Effect Controls

ƒ g
see_the_difference Comp 1 * g

ƒ	Write-on	Reset	About...
	Animation Presets	None	
	Brush Position	-⊹- 492.3 , 344.1	
	Color		
	Brush Size	24.6	
	Brush Hardness	56 %	
	Brush Opacity	100.0 %	
	Stroke Length (...	14.4	
	Brush Spacing (...	0.010	
	Paint Time Pro...	Color ▼	
	Brush Time Pro...	None ▼	
	Paint Style	Reveal Original Image ▼	

Scribble

This effect is a great way to color over a layer or fill it with something that looks a lot like licorice ropes gone mad. Okay so the description might make you think it's not very useful, but it's a surprisingly versatile effect and another way to create write-on effects or animated fills on letter or logos.

1 In order for the effect to work you need a mask. You can create it manually, or better yet, try the Auto-trace command (Layer>Auto-trace). Be sure to click the Preview box to see your results before creation.

2 Apply the results to a new layer.

3 On the resulting mask layer add the scribble effect by choosing Effect>Render>Scribble.

4 Adjust the angle, curviness, stroke width, and spacing.

5 Keyframe the Start or End to create an animated fill.

6 If desired change the Wiggle Type and Wiggles/Second.

7 Set Composite to On Transparent.

8 If desired, you can also use this layer as a track matte to wipe another layer on.

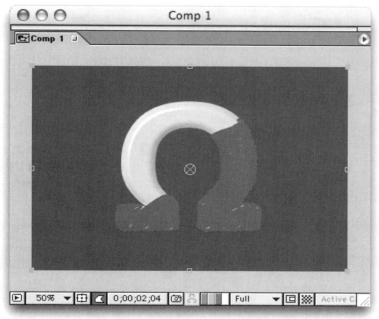

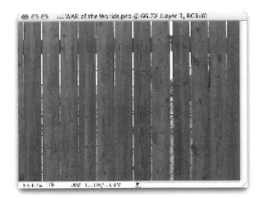

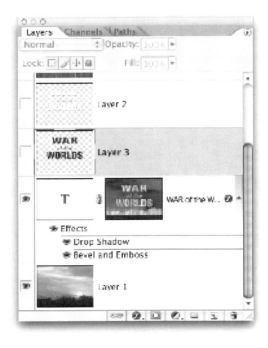

Distressed Type in Photoshop

Want to make editable vector type with distressed edges? You can by harnessing a photo texture and layer masks.

1 Typeset your words over your background layer(s).

2 Add a photo to your document with a lot of texture (in this case a photo of a wooden fence).

3 Desaturate the image by pressing Shift+Cmd+U (Shift+Ctrl+U).

4 Increase contrast in your photo through a combination of Levels Adjustments and Artistic filters such as Film Grain. Be sure to achieve a high contrast, yet allow gradual transitions.

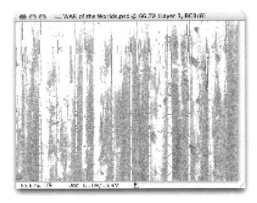

5 Switch to the Channels Palette and Cmd+click (Ctrl+Click) on the RGB composite channel to load a selection.

6 Switch back to your Layers Palette and turn off the texture layer's visibility icon.

7 Select your text channel and add a Layer mask by clicking on the Add layer mask button and the bottom of the Layers palette.

8 You may want to add a drop shadow or slight emboss to your text using layer styles. Experiment with blending modes as well.

9 If you want to distress the type further, keep going. Load the text layer by Cmd+Clicking (Ctrl+Clicking) on the text layer thumbnail.

10 Create a new empty layer and fill it with Black.

11 Choose Filter>Artistic>Cutout... to process the image further.

⑫ Switch to the Channels Palette and Cmd+Click (Ctrl+Click) on the RGB composite channel to load a selection.

⑬ Switch back to the Layers Palette and disable the Cutout layer.

⑭ Select your layer mask on your text layer and choose to fill with black. Your edges should erode more (if not, you can inverse the selection).

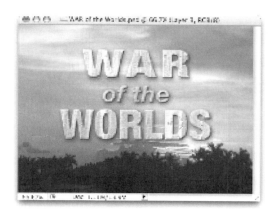

Quick Sunrays (and Other Repeating Patterns)

Sunrays are useful for lots of designs and the easiest way is in Adobe Illustrator.

❶ Create a long triangle with the point going down.

❷ Fill with a gradient or color if desired

❸ With the Rotate tool Opt+Click (Alt+Click) on the downward point.

❹ In the dialog box that pops up, the percentage of rotation that you enter will determine the number of rays that you have. Remember that a circle is 360° so if want 10 rays, you need to enter 36 for your percentage and choose Copy.

❺ Then Duplicate it 8 more times by hitting Cmd+D (Ctrl+D). This makes them evenly spaced.

Voila—you have a sunray. In After Effects you can add additional color or a gradient fill, and animate to your preference. This can also be used to create other tiles shapes as well.

By Jayse Hansen, http://www.xeler8r.com

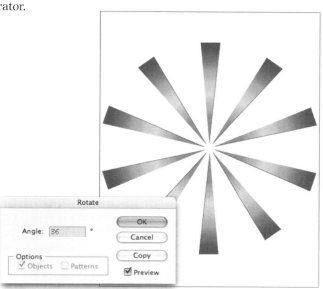

Adding Complexity to Your Designs Via Layering

Beginning designers often forget about the framing of their images. They forget what's "on top" of their imagery. Photography pros often vignette their images with darkened edges to enhance the focus on what's "inside" the picture. This same theory can be applied to motion graphics.

Here are the typical "top-layers" that can also be combined for your work.

A Grain Layer

Beginners are often afraid to lose the crystal clarity of what they worked so hard on – but often – it's that unreal sharpness that gives them away as amateurs.

This Can be Static – Photoshop

1 Fill a layer with 50% gray (Edit>Fill>50% Gray).

2 Run the Add-noise filter (Filter>Noise>Add Noise).

3 Set the filter to Gaussian and monochromatic and add a very tiny amount noise to your taste.

4 If desired, you can choose Edit>Fade immediately after running on a layer filled with 50% gray.

5 Set this layer to the Overlay blending mode.

This Can be Dynamic – After Effects

1 Add an adjustment layer to the top of your image.

2 Use the above technique but choose Effects>Noise & Grain>Noise.

3 Adjust the blending mode and opacity of the adjustment layer to get the right balance.

Darkened Edges Layer (or Power Window)

This is typically a very dark colored layer (never pure black—always use a more organic super-dark blue, burgundy or dark brown to fit your art instead).

❶ In After Effects, create a new solid layer that is filled with a dark color of your choice.

❷ Apply an oval mask or a rectangular mask (your choice).

❸ Set the mask to Subtract and feather the edges.

❹ Adjust the blending mode of the layer itself. Usually multiply or color burn with a reduced opacity works best.

Soft Glow Layer

As a quick polish, you can stylize your footage by adding a specular highlight adjustment layer.

❶ In After Effects, create a new adjustment layer.

❷ Add a fast blur to the adjustment layer. Try Effect>Blur>Fast Blur or CC Radial Fast Blur.

❸ Choose a healthy radius for the blur such as 15 or higher.

❹ Set this layer's blending mode to Soft Light, Overlay, or another blending mode of choice.

❺ Adjust the opacity to taste.

By Jayse Hansen, http://www.xeler8r.com

Leave Color Effect (After Effects)

A quick way to get the effect of one main color being saturated whilst the others are grayscale is using the Leave Color effect inside After Effects. Whether you're enhancing sports footage or sophisticated red dresses, the process is similar. Let's say you're trying to isolate the color red in a scene. Firstly, try to ensure that everything in your scene does not contain the color red, except for something like the girl's lips and dress. Now, it's important that you don't think "literally" red. Think "red" tones. Wood, for instance, will have many red tones. Try to surround your subject with opposite tones. It doesn't matter if they match—after all they will all become grays anyway.

image courtesy the American Diabetes Association

❶ Inside After Effects, apply the effect Stylize>Leave Color and use the eyedropper to pick the red in the scene.

❷ Set the Amount to Decolor to 100% and up the tolerance and Edge Softness in one-step increments until you get what you're after.

❸ You'll often find that setting the Match Colors setting to Hue works better than RGB.

❹ To enhance this single color, try adding an Adjustment layer with a Hue/Saturation Effect and pumping up the Saturation values.

Keeping skin tones is harder than keeping more vibrant primary colors like blue and red. You'll notice in *Sin City* when they are keeping skin tones that they also keep pretty much all the warm tones as well. For the other shots they had a distinct advantage: They filmed everything against a green screen, making it easy to control the colors and simply add in black and white backgrounds in post. If you're adventurous, you could do the same.

By Jayse Hansen, http://www.xeler8r.com

The Secret FREE Effects Book

How did we learn to use all of the effects? Easy, we read the book. You know, the book that explains how every parameter of every effect works.

What? You don't know about the book? Well, you own it. It's on your AE installation CD. Just pop it into your hard drive and navigate to the \AE6.5 Documentation\English folder. The book is an Adobe Acrobat file called help_effects.pdf. We recommend that you print it out, take it to a stationery shop, and pay a couple of bucks to have it bound. It may just prove to be the most valuable AE book you own.

- Among it other virtues, this is the only book that explains, in detail, how to use the five free (awesome) effects you downloaded when you registered your copy of AE at Adobe.com. You did download the free effects, didn't you? If not, reregister AE so you can grab them. You don't want to miss out on the fun of Card Wipe, Card Dance, Foam, Caustics, and Wave World.

- While you're printing the effects book, you might also want to print the Keylight and 3D Assistants manuals, which are also on the installation CD.

- Note: if you're missing your install CD, you can download the AE 5.5 version of the effects books here (it's almost exactly the same as the AE 6 book): http://www.adobe.com/products/aftereffects/zip/ae_effects_pdfs.zip.

Adobe·After Effects·

Adobe After Effects 5.5 Effect PDFs

The PDF files in this folder provide additional documentation for the effects that come with After Effects 5.5. Refer to the table on the following pages to determine the PDF that contains the information for a particular effect. The effect names are listed alphabetically in the first column. The second column gives the category name under which the effect can be found both in the After Effects Effect menu and in the PDF. The third column lists the name of the PDF that includes the effect information.

Effects listed in bold type are included in After Effects Production Bundle only. Effects listed with an asterisk are not included on the After Effects CD but can be downloaded from the Web free of charge after you register your copy of After Effects. Effects listed with two asterisks do not work with OS X and have been placed in a separate folder.

Visit the After Effects page of the Adobe Web site (http://www.adobe.com/products/aftereffects/main.html) to find additional information about After Effects including tutorials, and links to user groups and other resources.

ON THE SPOT

Getting it on the Air
Outputting Graphics to Tape, NLE, and Still Store

Well, it's the end of the book (or at least almost). What kind of hosts would we be if we didn't wrap this party up right. Working in Photoshop and After Effects is great, but those two programs are merely the beginning of your graphic's journey.

In a broadcast environment, you'll have several customers. Whether it's the Promotions Department who needs a graphic to cut into their Avid system, the News Department looking for something laid off to tape, or the Production Department calling for you to load something into the still store, someone always seems to need you.

This chapter will help smooth your graphic transitions and offer you some new ideas on moving things around.

Photo by Andi Hazelwood/iStockphoto

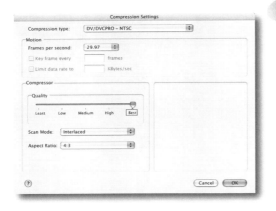

Pick the Right Codec

A codec is the method that a movie file is compressed and decompressed. Each NLE, clip server, and video board uses a particular codec. In order to quickly get your rendered animations into your NLE or other output device, it is recommended that you render with the device's particular codec. You select the codec for your render in the Format Options of the Output module. Many people will render with the Animation codec, but this will cause your NLE to need to render the animation once it is imported. (However, if you don't know what the destination system is, the Animation codec is a good one to use.) If you create animations for multiple systems, make sure that you have the codec for each target system installed, and render for the system you are sending the animation to.

Make Sure Your Fields Are in Order

Another critical setting in After Effects for animations that are going to video is the field order of the render. As you know, NTSC video is interlaced with one field displayed after another. If you render something in After Effects and don't field render, or you render with the wrong field order, you will notice a staggered jittery motion to the elements within your rendered clip. Different codecs use different field orders. In the render settings dialog in After Effects, make sure that you set the Field Render option to either Upper or Lower field first, depending on your NLE system. Check you NLE's documentation to find the correct field order for your system.

Here are a few:

- AVID ABVB – Upper Field First

- AVID Meridien or DNA – Lower Field First

- Digital Video – Lower Field First

- Media 100 – Lower Field First

I Thought Still Graphics are Supposed to Sit Still

Have you ever noticed that sometimes when your Photoshop images go to video, there is motion or flickering in portions of your image? This is a phenomenon known as field flicker and it is caused when fine horizontal, highly contrasting elements fall between horizontal scan lines in the video signal. If this happens to you, here is a quick fix.

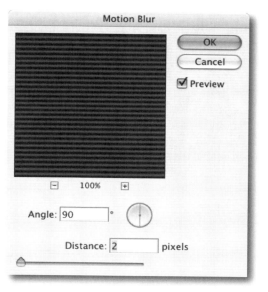

❶ Select the layer in your Photoshop document that is causing the flicker.

❷ Apply a 1-2 pixel motion blur (Filter>Blur>Motion Blur) with a 90° angle to the layer. This will push the bounds of the detail into the adjoining scan line, eliminating the flicker. You may need to increase the blur to 3 or more for really bad flicker issues.

- To avoid this problem in the first place, avoid creating horizontal lines in your images with a weight of 1 pixel. A weight of 3 will guarantee that you don't have any problems.

- If you are using Photoshop CS2 (or newer) be sure to load the Video Actions in your Actions palette. Run the Interlace Flicker Removal action as many times as needed.

Isn't Video 30 Frames Per Second?

Traditionally it has been, but in recent years the addition of cameras that are capable of shooting at 24fps have changed things a bit. If you are creating elements in After Effects for broadcast, many editors will work in 24fps until the end of the post phase, and then output a 30fps version for air. Always check with the editor you are working with and find out what frame rate they are editing in. If you do this up front, you won't be reworking and re-rendering elements down the road.

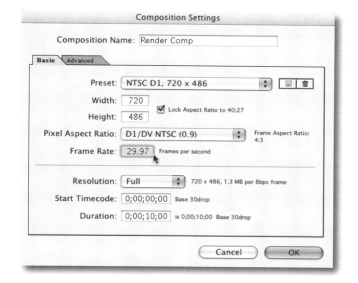

Photo by Laura Wile/iStockphoto

Adding Text in Your CG

This is not always possible, but if you are outputting your Photoshop graphics on a CG system, we recommend using Photoshop for your background elements and textures, and then applying text to them in your CG. This allows for much more flexibility when text changes are necessary. Text is quickly edited in a CG, and even though Photoshop makes quick and easy text changes, those extra few seconds that you save going to and from Photoshop for text changes can make the difference between something getting on air or not.

Check Your Colors

Have you ever noticed that after you finely tune your images to be exactly the shade the client wants, they change completely when they go out to video? This is caused by the different color gamuts used by your computer monitor and NTSC video. It is inevitable that this is going to happen, but it is possible to work out color issues early in the process. The best way to deal with this problem is to work in Photoshop and After Effects on a video monitor where you can preview your work on an NTSC monitor. Here are a few solutions that provide this functionality.

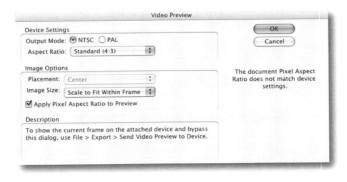

- Use the new built-in Send video preview to device that is found under File>Export. This will output the image you currently have active in Photoshop to a DV video device. You can set up a variety of output options related to scaling, 16x9, and video format under File>Export>Video preview.

- Use a third-party tool called Echo Fire created by Synthetic Aperture. This plug-in provides the same functionality as the built-in export feature, but adds the ability to view a waveform monitor and vector scope that analyzes your image. Plus, they have support for After Effects.

- Purchase a video card for your system such as one made by DigitalVoodoo, BlueFish444, BlackMagic, or AJA. These cards no only give you video I/O for your editing system, but they also allow you to extend your desktop to the card and work right on a video display.

Two Is Better Than One

We recommend working with a 2 file system in Photoshop. Never flatten your Photoshop file just so you can send it to your video system. File management is the key to a smooth workflow. For every project, here are a few must-do's!

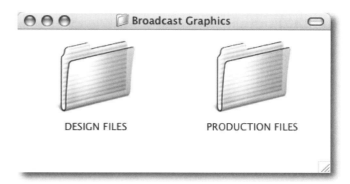

DESIGN FILES   PRODUCTION FILES

- Always keep a design file (layered Photoshop file) for content or layout changes.

- Always keep a production file (flattened TARGA or TIFF file) that you send to your video system.

- Organize your files in folders based on project and file type (design or production).

The Key to Video Graphics (Pun Intended!)

Alpha channels are single most important part of your images. Without them, the best-designed lower third in the world is useless. Make sure that your images that will be keyed have an alpha channel associated with them.

- We recommend using TARGA files for the files that get sent to a video device.

- Once the alpha channel is created, save the TARGA file as a 32 bits/pixel file. This assures that the graphic will save the alpha channel within the file.

- Know what type of alpha channel your system wants. Different systems interpret alpha channels differently; some key out black, others white. Provide your system with the right type of alpha so that you don't have to invert it every time you import an image.

- Save full screen images as 24 bits/pixel images. Even though saving them at 32 bits/pixel will make them work correctly when they go live, many still store systems will designate them as keyable graphics if they detect an alpha channel. This just adds confusion when you don't need any.

221

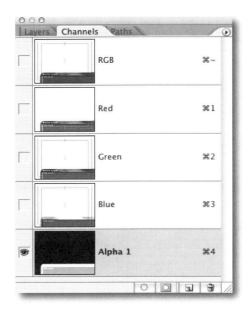

Alpha Channel Basics

Alpha channels are created by making a selection of all of the combined layers in your image, and creating a new channel in the Channels palette from this selection. Here are some things to know about alpha channels.

- If you have more than one extra channel in the Channels palette, Photoshop will not allow you to save an alpha channel. Make sure you only have one.

- Making changes to your image in terms of text changes, layer placement, or new image content that changes the overall transparent area of your image will change the alpha channel that is needed to key that graphic. Get into the habit of creating a new alpha channel before saving your production file for your NLE. This will help you avoid a return trip to Photoshop to fix a bad alpha.

- If your video system wants an inverted alpha, you can create a standard alpha channel where black is keyed out. Then select the new alpha channel and press Cmd-I (Ctrl-I) to invert it.

Premultiplied Alpha Channels

A premultiplied alpha channel is an alpha channel that perfectly matches the outline of the images that it is trying to key out. The potential problem that you run into with premultiplied alphas is that as the image uses anti-aliasing to smooth its edges, you introduce the background color of the image into the edges of your artwork.

After Effects and other video applications allow you to set what color the background of your images are so that they can un-multiply that color from the edges of your graphic. If you fail to do this, you will get an unintended halo or glow effect around your image when it is keyed.

In After Effects, this option appears when you import images with alpha channels. You can also access it under File>Interpret Footage>Main. This needs to be set for all images that rely on alpha channels for keying. The color that you want to select is the color of the background of the image.

Give It to Me Straight

By nature, Photoshop does not easily create straight alpha channels for you. However, once you have a keyable image that you created in Photoshop, you can open that image in After Effects and it can render a version of the image out that has a straight alpha channel. This is only needed if your video system or NLE cannot properly interpret a pre-multiplied alpha channel.

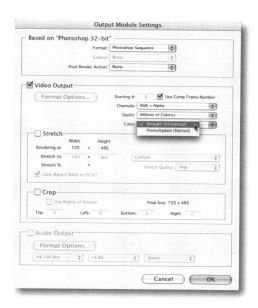

1 Import the image with alpha into After Effects.

2 Tell After Effects that the image has a premultiplied alpha and choose the background color of the image.

3 Create a new composition and place the image in it.

4 Select Composition>Save Frame As>File.

5 Change the video output color setting in the output module to Straight (unmated).

6 Render the image. You now have an image with a straight alpha channel that will solve the problem if you are having issues with dark edges around your graphic, or drop shadows that appear to have a white edge to them.

Automatic Alpha Channels

If you need an alpha channel fast, then Photoshop CS2 has got you covered. Be sure to check out the new Video Actions from the submenu of the Actions palette. You'll find two actions that are well suited for all video pros.

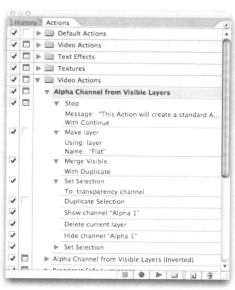

1 Turn off the visibility for all layers that do not belong in the final graphic including the Background layer and Safe Title Overlay.

2 Run either the Alpha Channel from Visible Layers or the Alpha Channel from Visible Layers (inverted) depending on your systems needs. Avid editors will need to use the inverted option.

3 Save the final graphic in a format that supports embedded alpha channels such as PICT, TIFF, or TARGA.

Pixel Aspect Ratios

Have you ever noticed that sometimes graphics end up looking stretched vertically on a video monitor when they looked fine on your computer monitor? Surely you have heard something about non-square pixels. We recommend that you always work off video graphics in Photoshop as non-square pixel images. Here's how.

- When creating a new document, make sure to choose a video preset. These all have the correct pixel aspect ratio assigned to them.

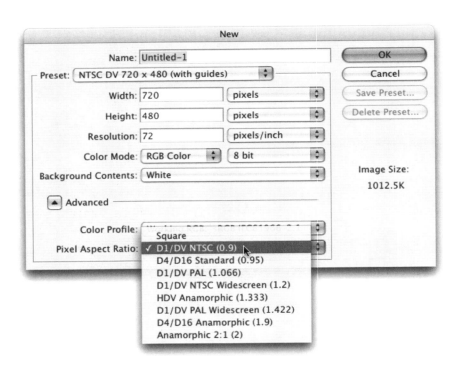

- When you bring a video still into Photoshop, change its pixel aspect ratio to the correct setting based on your video format. Image>Pixel Aspect Ratio. Failing to do so will cause your text and other tools to create square pixel content.

- Don't open a digital photo and change its pixel aspect ratio to a video ratio. This will make the stretching worse. Always create a new image that has a non-square pixel aspect ratio and place, paste, or move your photos into the non-square pixel canvas.

Testing an Alpha Channel in Real Time

If you have a DigitalVoodoo, BlueFish444, or another card that supports Photoshop transparency, you can tell Photoshop to output its transparency as an alpha channel to a separate output on the card.

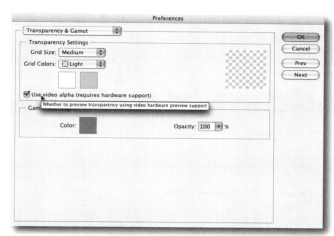

- This is accomplished by opening the Transparency & Gamut preference in Photoshop's preferences window.

- Check the Use video alpha box.

- You will notice that the transparent areas in Photoshop turn gray, and the color areas of your image fatten up. This is allowing Photoshop to output the transparent area as an actual alpha channel to your video card, and makes it a straight (as opposed to a premulitplied) key.

- Drag your Photoshop canvas from your main monitor to the video second monitor, which is your video output.

- Maximize the canvas to 100% using Cmd-Option-0 (Ctrl-Alt-0)

- Toggle to full screen mode (F).

You can now run this output right into a switcher and see how your graphics key in real time while you are editing them.

Photoshop Layers Into Your NLE

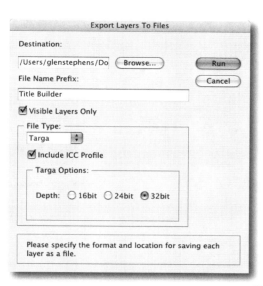

Even though most NLEs boast support for layered Photoshop files, they don't all support the layer styles, text layers, or adjustment layers that reside in your document. The fastest and easiest way to get layered Photoshop files into your NLE is to use the File>Scripts>Export Layers to Files script. This will save each layer with its layer style and adjustment layers applied to a new, flattened Photoshop document with transparency. You can now bring these files into your NLE and reassemble the order for animation. If you are not planning on animating the image, the simply send it a flattened TARGA file that is the a composite of the entire image.

Black and White Are Not So Black and White

If you find your image clipped in the brightest and darkest areas of your image, you are probably working on a video system that deals with video black and white at a different level than Photoshop.

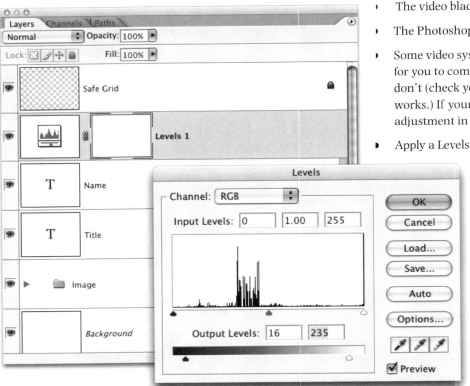

- The video black to white range is 16-235

- The Photoshop black to white range is 0-255

- Some video systems make the conversion in your graphics for you to compensate for the different ranges. But some don't (check your manual to find out how your system works.) If yours doesn't here is how you make the adjustment in Photoshop.

- Apply a Levels adjustment layer to the top of your document.

  - Set the output black level to 16

  - Set the output white level to 235

You can turn this layer off while you are designing, but when you are ready to save a file for your video system, make sure that you turn the adjustment layer on.

Safe Grids Are for You as a Designer

If you are using the built-in guides in Photoshop as your safe grid, you are pretty much bullet proof on this. If you are using a layer for your safe grid, always double check to make sure that you hide this layer before you save a file for your video system. Nothing is more frustrating than showing your client a final video with graphics that have safe grids on them. Here is a way to make sure that it gets hidden every time you save the image.

- Always name the safe grid layer the same name.

- Create an action that hides that layer.

- Create a script event manager event that runs this script each time the image is saved.

Most third-party solutions that rely on safe grid layers, such as Tools for Television PRO, manage this for you as well.

The Ever Changing World of HD

If you have been charged with the task of creating graphics for an HD production, here is a tip that will make your images reusable and safe from format changes. It is a good idea to get into the habit of creating all of your HD images at 1920x1080. Even if your production is for a 1280x720 format, both standards are 16x9. If your production team decides at a later point in time to master at 1080i, you are covered. If they decide to distribute a 720p version, simply have a batch action ready to resize your 1080 images to the 720 format. The aspect ratios are the same, so you won't loose anything in terms of image quality. This is smart designing. Be prepared for anything, don't duplicate your efforts.

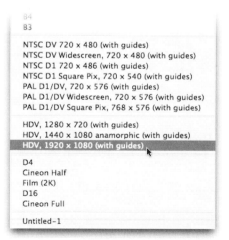

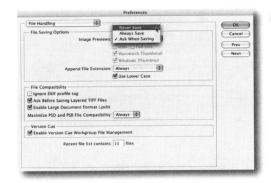

Faster Transfers to a Still Store

Many still stores and graphics systems require that you use an FTP protocol to transfer the files to them. If you are lucky enough to have a gigabit network, these transfers happen quickly. If you are running a slower network, or just want to squeeze a little more performance out of your FTP, you can turn off the image icon and thumbnails on your files.

1 Open Photoshop's preferences.

2 Select the file handling options.

3 Change the preview settings either to Never or Ask When Saving.

By disabling the icon and thumbnails, you will decrease the size of your files, making your ftp transfers lean and mean.

Splitting the Alpha Channel in After Effects

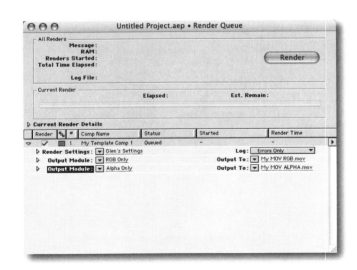

If you need to output image and alpha in separate files from After Effects, you need to do it with two output modules.

1 Create an output module template that has a video output set to RGB.

2 Create an output module template that has a video output set to Alpha.

3 Send your animation to the render queue.

4 Choose the RGB output module template for the default output module.

5 Add another output module, and assign it to your Alpha output module template.

Of course you can render a file with both RGB and alpha in the same file by setting the video output to RGB+Alpha, but if you need two files this is the ticket.

Splitting the Alpha Channel in Photoshop

Some video systems require that your alpha channel and graphic be in separate files. There is not an automatic way to do this in Photoshop, however you can create an action that will do this for you.

Here are the rough steps to the action.

1. Select the Alpha 1 channel in the Channels palette in the document.

2. Select all Cmd-A (Ctrl-A).

3. Copy the channel to the clipboard.

4. Duplicate the document (Image>Duplicate).

5. Flatten the new document.

6. Paste the clipboard to the new document.

7. Flatten again.

8. Save as a targa file 24 bit/pixel.

9. Close the duplicated document.

Now you can create a Script Event Manager event that calls this action each time you save a file. Instant alpha without any thought on your part.

EDITED BY RICHARD HARRINGTON

Learn real-world techniques for using After Effects in commercial video and film projects straight from the pros. Twelve tutorials showcase a wide range of projects, from low-budget commercials to big screen film trailers, created for a client budget of $10,000 or less. The companion DVD contains the source files required for you to replicate the techniques as well as Apple QuickTime presentations of the final projects. Available September 2005

$44.95, 4-color softcover with DVD, 240 pages, ISBN 1-57820-267-1

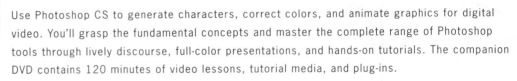

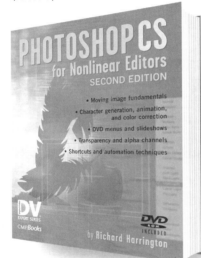

PHOTOSHOP CS FOR NONLINEAR EDITORS, 2ND EDITION RICHARD HARRINGTON

Use Photoshop CS to generate characters, correct colors, and animate graphics for digital video. You'll grasp the fundamental concepts and master the complete range of Photoshop tools through lively discourse, full-color presentations, and hands-on tutorials. The companion DVD contains 120 minutes of video lessons, tutorial media, and plug-ins.

$54.95, 4-color softcover with DVD, 310 pages, ISBN 1-57820-237-X

AFTER EFFECTS ON THE SPOT RICHARD HARRINGTON, RACHEL MAX, MARCUS GEDULD

Packed with more than 400 expert techniques, this book clearly illustrates the essential methods that pros use to get the job done with After Effects. Experienced motion graphic artists and novices alike discover an invaluable reference filled with ways to improve efficiency and creativity.

$27.95, Softcover, 288 pages, ISBN 1-57820-239-6